CHARA'S STORY

TRYING TO GET TO A PLACE CALLED "PRETTY"

HOW I DISCOVERED THE TRUTH ABOUT BEAUTY

CHARA MCGILL

Copyright © 2019 by Chara McGill
All rights reserved. This book or any portion thereof
may not be reproduced or used in any manner whatsoever
without the express written permission of the publisher
except for the use of brief quotations in a book review.

The events and conversations in this book have been set down
to the best of the author's ability, although some names and
details have been changed to protect the privacy of individuals.
*No liability is assumed for damages that may result
from the use of information contained within.*

Printed in the United States of America

First printing, 2019.

ISBN 978-1-7334857-0-8 (e-book)
ISBN 978-1-7334857-1-5 (Paperback)
ISBN 978-1-7334857-2-2 (Hardcover)

Email: Chara@TheTruthAboutBeauty.me

DEDICATION

Because my desire is to make the truth about beauty the cultural norm, this book is dedicated to the next generation.

CONTENTS

Title Page
Copyright
Dedication
Introduction   1
Part One   5
Chapter 1   6
Chapter 2   12
Chapter 3   19
Chapter 4   26
Chapter 5   31
Chapter 6   39
Chapter 7   45
Chapter 8   52
Chapter 9   59
Chapter 10   63
Part Two   69
Chapter 11   70
Chapter 12   76
Chapter 13   84
Chapter 14   89
Chapter 15   95

Chapter 16	101
Chapter 17	111
Chapter 18	123
Chapter 19	134
Chapter 20	148
ACKNOWLEDGMENTS	150

INTRODUCTION

Recently, I and three college students from the University of Georgia (UGA) sat down with a room of hyper sixth grade girls at a local Boys & Girls Club. I had no idea the conversation would become so deep so quickly. After all, it was our first session. I had recruited the college students to facilitate an antibullying program associated with Girl Scouts called *Be a Friend First*." It would be my first time seeing these young adults and sixth graders interact with one another. The UGA students shared their stories of being bullied and how they handled it. The teens listened intently, and toward the end of the session, they begged to share their experiences. We'd planned for the teen girls to share their stories during the next session. However, they were so persistent in asking to do so right then that we obliged and gave them the floor. One young lady was especially persistent; she spoke first. We were not prepared for what she told us.

"So last year, I had a best friend who was always being teased, and she cried a lot," she began. "I was talking to her about how she should ignore the bullies who were teasing her. I begged her to learn to ignore them, and I talked with her daily. I knew she was having a hard time, so I did everything that I could to make her feel supported. One day, everybody was looking for her at school and couldn't find her. They even came in my classroom and asked me if I had seen her. I said, 'No.' I then asked my teacher if I could go to the bathroom. I literally was just going to use the bathroom, not thinking of nothing. I walked in, and I pulled on the stall door. There she was, hanging, with something tied around her neck, at the top of the stall."

We all gasped. We needed a moment to breathe after what we'd just heard. To our relief, she had found her friend in time to save her life. We asked what her friend was being bullied about and why she wanted to kill herself. Her response was "her appearance." By session's end, many more teens admitted they'd contemplated or attempted suicide due to negative body image concerns or being shamed for their looks. One girl mentioned she was being teased because her teeth were crooked, and she had tried to kill herself twice. Keep in mind, we *weren't* talking to high school students. We were talking to sixth graders who had contemplated or attempted killing themselves. We sat stunned at the stories being shared with us. We knew body image was a huge struggle for teens; we just didn't know how bad the problem was.

Researchers have noted that negative body image issues among young girls is a cultural norm.[1] In the United States, many girls and women of various ages are dealing with body image dissatisfaction and a negative self-image.[2] This is closely linked to low self-esteem, which can lead to eating disorders, depression, anxiety, substance abuse, and suicidal thoughts.[3] I know these emotions all too well.

I, too, was secretly a part of these statistics, beginning at the age of seven. At twenty-four, with a fear of never measuring up to society's beauty standards, I became suicidal. My story recounts my personal struggle and journey to reach a place called *Pretty*. At times this journey left me hopeless and confused. The negative body image I developed as a child grew to a massive mental monster that would rear its ugly head in my young adult years, causing missed opportunities, brokenness, and the wasting of energy I desperately needed to fulfill my purpose in life.

I didn't think I would make it out of that particular season in my life alive. To survive, I went on a journey to discover the truth about beauty, and in an unexpected way, I found it.

You see, I discovered *real* beauty in, literally, the ugliest season of my life. It changed me. I found life again. I found real beauty. I found me.

When you read my story, you will uncover, just as I did, the *truth* about beauty, despite what society portrays. I will show when and how the root of my insecurities began to take hold and how my life experiences fueled my negative thoughts of myself. You will read about my intense struggle to become pretty and how I finally reached that place, only to have the unthinkable happen to me—a girl who wanted to be physically perfect. I'm grateful to have made it through the process, and I don't take it for granted. On my journey, I discovered five foundational keys to freedom from a negative self-image. By reading this book, you too will learn how you can start your journey to freedom from a negative self-image.

Why is it important to discover the *truth* about beauty? In a nutshell, this truth brings forth fulfillment and ends the cycle of discontentment and body image dissatisfaction. It dispels every lie you hear that goes against the truth of your beauty. You will start to see yourself in a positive light, despite any physical imperfection. Knowing the truth about beauty can set you free from a negative self-image. It is the truth that sets us all free.

DISCLAIMER: *I am not a critic of the medication/s that I discuss in this book. I am in no way against medical procedures or medicines. I can only speak to my own story, and I present it to you as it occurred.*

PART ONE

CHAPTER 1

JUST CHARA

I knocked on his door, impatient to see him. I was excited and nervous. He'd invited me to his dorm room. Anytime we got together, we laughed, talked, and flirted. Yes, I liked him, and I knew that he liked me too. However, I knew I couldn't be his girlfriend, and when he opened the door, there was yet another confirmation as to why. I yelled, "Hey, my friend! You finally came to the door, huh?" He looked at me like I was crazy, and I couldn't figure out why. So I asked him, "What's wrong with you? Why are you looking at me like that?"

His response was something I should have anticipated. He asked, "Why are you dressed in jogging pants and a T-shirt? And why is your hair in a bun?"

I pretended to ignore his comments and walked in his dorm room to check out his creative environment.

But he insisted on explaining. "You look better dressed in tight clothes, with your hair down. Don't you know that? You got a bangin' body, and you're hidin' it."

I turned around, looked him in the eye, and said, "You see, that's why I can't be your girl. You want perfection, and I can't give that to you."

Seeing that I was serious, he answered back, "I'm just playin', girl. But I'm just saying, you have a nice body, and you have long, beautiful hair. You should show it off is all I'm saying."

There were many times I had to remind him that he *wasn't* my boyfriend—or maybe I had to remind *myself* that he wasn't my boyfriend. But who was I kidding? I really liked him. Within two minutes of our conversation, the cute little bun on the top of my head was no more. I slowly started taking the pins out of my hair to let it hang down my back. I secretly wanted to please him and have him continue to like me. From that point on, whenever I was around him, I wore formfitting clothes and let my hair hang down just the way he liked.

I remember the first day I saw him. He was definitely my type, but at first I didn't even consider being his friend because he was so handsome. But one day I saw him walking around campus, going in circles, and looking down at a little sheet of paper. I gathered up my courage, approached him, and asked if he needed help. He smiled as he realized he looked lost. I pointed him in the right direction, and he looked back with a smile as he walked to his class. From that day on, we spoke to each other in passing. I always wanted to talk to him, but I was too scared to stop him again. One day he approached me and asked for my name and number. Talk about being giggly—I was so happy.

We got to know each other over time. I considered him a friend but liked him more than that. In addition to being handsome, he was a really popular guy. We hung out together on our college campus all the time, and sometimes we did our homework together. Well, honestly, *I* did *his* homework.

He constantly asked me to be his girlfriend, but I opted only to be his friend. I was very insecure and felt that to be with someone so handsome, I had to be perfect. Plus, he confirmed my insecurities with his superficial comments about what he liked in women. He was so into a woman's figure and her appearance. This superficial mind-set consumed him. We joked about it a lot. But the truth was that beauty according to him meant being physically perfect: slim waist and body, beautiful teeth, long and flowing hair, supple lips, manicured nails—even your feet had to be on point.

This notion of beauty wasn't at all foreign to me, though. It was the norm to try to reach for in my world. It's how my peers and I had viewed beauty since childhood. Just like him. It's what we were all trying to measure up to. I guess that's why his mind-set wasn't surprising to me.

When we talked about finding him the "right one," I would often say that if he did find his Barbie, he could easily be her Ken. So, for the duration of this book, I will refer to him as my friend Ken.

My peers would approach me all the time, baffled as to why we weren't a couple, but I felt too insecure to be in that kind of relationship with him. My desire to be beautiful had *everything* to do with my efforts to measure up to people like Ken. But, actually, nothing was wrong with me. I had beautiful, long hair; perfect skin; nice teeth; and I was a size 2. Ken loved my look, but I didn't. I felt I couldn't compare with other girls I deemed prettier.

I had always dreamed of a guy like Ken being interested in me. I remember being in middle school, daydreaming about a really handsome guy all the girls wanted, but he only wanted me. And since he only wanted me, then I must be pretty, right? That daydream became my reality. Ken liked me. But for some reason, I still didn't feel pretty enough. I didn't feel perfect, and I knew he wanted perfection.

Girls flirted with Ken all the time, and he enjoyed the attention. He would flirt with me too, but I never took him seriously because I knew he liked me physically more than anything else. He always complimented me on my hair. It was longer than most girls' hair, and it was my own—no extensions. I loved my hair. As an African American, it was a big deal. Hair extensions weren't as popular back in my college days and weren't as easily accessible. He would say, "Chara, you are so pretty, but don't ever cut your hair." That phrase was something I should have interpreted more closely. It would eventually prove to show his true colors.

While attending college, I began working on a theatrical production I wrote to build a scholarship fund. I became extremely busy with the production, and it began to stress me out. Ken noticed the change and didn't come around as often. We were still friends but didn't see each other nearly as much as I wanted. My college work had also gotten pretty stressful because my graduation date was so close to my production dates. I was working tirelessly, and the stress started to consume me. My hair was always a mess, and I looked unkempt half the time. It got so intense that I started taking specific vitamins to help with the anxiety.

I needed to calm down. I needed an outlet—bad. I decided to go see Ken. I knew he'd make me laugh and help me relax. Knowing Ken and his expectations, though, I first needed to get my hair done. I could not show up at his place with a messy bun on my head. So I booked a hair appointment.

As usual, my beautician placed chemicals on my hair to straighten out the roots. At that time, hair treatments for African American women came via a simple yet (unknown to us) dangerous process, in which strong chemicals were applied to the roots of the hair to straighten out any coils or curls. This was called "getting a perm." It was routine for me, so I didn't expect anything different. I expected to have healthy but, most of all, long and straightened hair, so I could go see my friend in mint condition.

But something terrible happened, something that I didn't expect at all. I heard my beautician, who was standing over me as my head rested in the shampoo bowl, cry out in fear, "Oh my God!" My hair had started to fall out as she was rinsing out the chemicals. I immediately grabbed my hair only to have half of it fall into my hands. I jumped up from the shampoo chair, screamed, and started walking away. Where I was going to go, I had no clue. I then started running around the shop, screaming. I was confused and devastated. My hairstylist dashed from behind the shampoo bowl, grabbed me, and said, "Calm down, calm down, let me continue to wash it out." She guided me back to the shampoo bowl and sat me down. As she continued rinsing the chemicals from my hair, I could feel strands leaving my scalp. I was horrified. I cried and screamed the entire time.

That day I lost 70 percent of my hair. My beautician had to cut my hair above my ears to cover the bald spots. She told me that cutting my hair would also help the process of growing healthy hair all over again. The whole ordeal was like the scene from the Tina Turner movie *What's Love Got to Do with It*, where the same thing happened to Ms. Turner—except I had no wig to cover my bald spots. It was a horrifying day for me, a day I wanted to forget. I cried all night because I loved my hair and felt that most of my beauty left me that day. My hair gave me confidence. It was something most others around me didn't have. My hair made me stand out—or at least I thought so. It defined me, and now that it was gone, I was devastated.

Stuck wearing short, thin hair, I wanted to hide from the world until it grew back. I felt ugly and incomplete. I especially wanted to hide from Ken. What would he say? How would he treat me? My plan was to at least hide from *him* for a while. As much as I wanted to stay indoors and not go to class, I had no choice. I had to deal with my new look, because, after all, graduation was just around the corner. So I hid in the one place I felt Ken would never enter: the campus library. I avoided his calls and stopped going to our usual hangout spots. My plan worked, but only for a while. The library became everybody's hangout spot during finals, and sure enough, while I was sitting in my usual little cubbyhole area one day, Ken found me.

"Chara, is that you?" Bracing myself for the uncomfortable conversation that was about to take place, I looked up with a smile. Brows scrunched together, he frowned and looked at me in shock, "Oh my goodness! Why did you cut your hair?" His face was all twisted; he looked totally confused. Before I could even explain what had happened, he said, "You were such a beautiful, dark-skinned girl. You walked around with this beautiful, nice hair blowing in the wind. You should have never cut your hair because now you're just… you're just… just Chara."

Without giving me a chance to say anything, he left. I guess that was his way of telling me to have a nice life, and that I was no longer pretty enough to hang with him. We never hung out again in college. I knew I'd lost my friend—not because something had happened to him but because I wasn't the picture-perfect girl he once knew. To him I was now average, and he didn't want average.

CHAPTER 2

DARK AND UGLY

I sat in the campus library unable to study and unable to focus on my research paper. Ken's voice kept replaying in my head: "You're just… just Chara." I felt numb. I had to ask myself, "How did I get here?" Why was I hanging around a guy that I *knew* only liked me for my appearance? Thinking back to the day he saw me in joggers and a T-shirt, I thought, "What was wrong with me wearing comfortable clothing? Why did I continuously hang out with such a superficial guy?" I pondered and pondered why I allowed someone like him into my inner circle to crush the little self-esteem I had.

Ken's statement "You're just Chara" would haunt me for years. I had begun to believe that me without makeup wasn't good enough, me without fitted clothing or long hair just wasn't good enough. What caused me to think like this? What caused me to see myself as average? Suddenly, I realized that this mind-set had developed way before I met Ken. It was the reason I'd allowed him into my life and the reason I'd never kicked him out. He merely fueled my way of thinking, in which I saw myself as average—a mind-set that started one day in third grade. My thoughts drifted back to that day.

The Third Grade

It was a quiet morning. All twenty-one third graders

sat cooperatively completing our assignments. It was "National School Lunch Week," and parents were invited to eat lunch with us at our elementary school. All week, everyone would stop working and look up each time there was a knock at the door. All you could hear were whispers from anxious third graders, trying to guess whose parent belonged to whom. Nobody wanted to be the laughingstock of the bunch, and many students were praying their parents didn't come in looking crazy. Unfortunately, some parents showed up and totally embarrassed their kids in one way or another. I guess they didn't understand just how cruel third graders could be to one another. If your parents looked weird or were dressed funny, according to our little third-grade standards at the time, you would be talked about in the worst way.

It was Friday, the last day of National School Lunch Week. The traffic of parents had slowed down. But as we sat quietly doing our work, there was one more knock on the door. A younger-looking, light-skinned lady walked into our classroom, wearing a pretty pink, flowing dress, with a pink belt around her waist to accentuate her outfit. I looked up and smiled. The teacher walked over to talk with her, and the whispers began. Everybody wanted to know whose mom she was.

Two classmates, one in front of me and one behind, commented on her beauty. I responded—loudly enough for my section of peers to hear— "That's my mom." I was happy they were complimenting my mother.

But then one girl shouted, "That's not your mom! You're dark, and your mom is light skinned and pretty." Laughter and teasing burst out. It seemed as if their words were broadcast through the loudspeaker. "How can that pretty lady be your mother?" they said.

Puzzled and unnerved, I tried to defend myself, but by this time, the teacher had gathered the class in order and called my name. "Chara, your mother wants to take you to the cafeteria early and sit with you, so she can get back to work."

I got up from my seat and walked toward her. She had the

biggest smile on her face. She reached down to hug me, unaware that a battle had just started to break out in my mind.

She was as happy to see me as I was to see her; Mom didn't make visits to our school often. This was a special occasion for me and my twin sister (whom she had also come to see). As we walked to the cafeteria, I studied her beautiful complexion, soft hair, and exquisite smile. I replayed the voices of my classmates in my head: "You're dark, and your mom is light skinned and pretty." As we sat face-to-face, I examined my skin, then examined more of my mother's. I'd never realized I was a darker skin tone than her. Looking back, I don't know why I didn't shrug my shoulders and ignore their comments. I guess I wasn't wired that way, and my self-esteem just wasn't built to the point where I could take those kinds of remarks and be okay.

As I sat across from my mom in the school cafeteria, I tried my best to hold back tears. "God, why did you make my mom pretty and me so dark? Why couldn't I be light skinned and pretty like my mother?" Then guilt set it. I thought to myself, "My mother was the best-looking mom that came to the school. I should feel proud, not ashamed."

As we prepared to leave the lunchroom, my classmates walked in and pointed at us, still teasing me for being darker than my mom. She had no clue about what they'd said nor about my new internal battle. But because I now knew myself to be darker than my mom, I felt I was dark and ugly. (For years, this was my mind-set, and my mother wouldn't learn of it until my young-adult years.)

We finished lunch, and she kissed me goodbye. When I rejoined my classmates, the cruel words continued: "You got lucky for that lady to be your mom; you must be adopted."

My peers never actually said I was ugly; they just called me "dark" and my mom "light skinned" and "pretty." But there was an unspoken meaning: often, in my culture, a darker skin tone was deemed ugly. Even in elementary school, I noticed how African American boys liked and accepted lighter-skinned African American girls. Women and girls in the media, particularly in the 1980s, were of a lighter complexion and were presented as the standard for beauty. Books and literature showed me how the enslavement of African Americans and injustice toward them bred a mind-set of indignation and even hatred toward people with dark skin. During slavery, individuals with lighter skin tones were often brought out of the fields to work in the households of their slave masters. It was as if being of a darker complexion was a curse.

That week I continued contemplating whether I was really "dark and ugly." What happened next seemed to solidify what I already was beginning to believe. My twin sister and I were normally late for school for some reason, and Bee—my twin sister's best friend and one of the prettiest girls in the school—arrived around the same time we did. One day, as Bee and I walked in late as usual, the boys started whistling and flirting. My seat happened to be near the teacher. As I settled in, I overheard my teacher's conversation with her assistant. Her assistant said, "Oooh, Chara has some admirers." My teacher responded, "Please, they weren't whistling at *her*. They were whistling at Bee. She's light skinned and pretty."

I looked up in shock. There was that phrase again: "light skinned and pretty." Crushed and in disbelief, I thought, "Not my teacher too!" This really hurt. Why couldn't their whistles be for me? How did she know they didn't like me too? In that moment, it was as if my teacher confirmed the ugly truth: I was dark and ugly.

Am I Ugly?

How could I get prettier? That became my mission. That became my journey. I wanted to measure up, to be pretty—like Bee and like my own mother, who were beautiful in the eyes of my peers.

By seventh grade, my "dark and ugly syndrome" had grown. But as a young girl, I'd figured something out. If you had dark skin and wanted to be accepted, you had to have a nice butt and big breasts. Guess whose breasts grew in the seventh grade? I remember a guy calling me Dolly Parton. I didn't know who she was, and the internet was not... well, I'd give away my age if I went into further details. I will say this, though: I couldn't click on a social media page to figure out who she was; I was just told by one of my male peers that she was a pretty country singer with really big breasts.

So, of course, my next move was to accentuate my boobs! I remember sneaking tighter shirts into my book bag. My parents were very observant, and my dad noticed that when my mom took us shopping, I'd pick shirts smaller than my actual size. I remember him asking me, "What is wrong with you?" I never spoke of my struggle of feeling insecure. I didn't even know I *was* insecure. I just wanted to be accepted by guys at school—thought of as pretty, not ugly. I wanted to prove to myself that I was pretty. Wasn't this how girls measured our worth? "If he likes me, I'm pretty. If he thinks I'm cute, I'm accepted."

Even though I now know the truth about beauty, let's stop and think: Why do females get butt injections, breast implants, or any other body enhancements? Is it really so we can admire our body parts in the mirror? We may even think this behavior is normal and okay. We say we do it for ourselves, but are we really? Think about it. If you were the only person on earth, would you care to inject something into a part of your body to make it bigger?

As a young girl, society told me that if a boy liked me, then I was pretty. So, I felt pretty when I got attention from boys. Wearing fitted shirts got me attention, and attention is key to an insecure girl. It's her way of measuring her worth.

The 8th Grade

My experience in third grade affected me greatly, but a later experience in eighth grade solidified my unhealthy body image. As I sat in the campus library still, I continued to reflect back. One particular event stood out to me. It was a hot and humid day, our eighth-grade class was returning from a field trip. We were all standing in line, waiting to load the bus. As each girl boarded, several hormone-raging boys, who looked like they should have graduated high school already, would cheer and applaud if the girl was attractive and invite her to sit in the back with them. If she was unattractive, they would boo and criticize her, forcing her to sit closer to the front.

When I realized what was happening, I started feeling like I was about to face the judgment seat. My friends and I just wanted to get on the bus. I looked around, hoping to be rescued by my teacher, any teacher, but there were none to be found. In my mind, I was dark and ugly, but since my breasts were big and I had long hair, maybe, just maybe, I'd be invited to the back of the bus. More than anything, though, I just didn't want to be criticized. I walked closer and closer to the bus. It was finally my turn. Step one, step two, step three. What would they say about me?

My experience was quite different from the other girls. As soon as I stepped on the bus, one guy started booing. Another guy told him to stop. He said, "She's not ugly; she's good, she's good. Nice body." Another guy said, "Yeah, she all right. She can sit in the middle." But before they could invite me to the back or the middle, I had already found my seat closer to the front. I exhaled, thinking about what their comments meant.

I looked around, and some girls actually had tears in their eyes. Others just screamed back, "Boo you, boy!" Some gladly went to the back; others pretended not to care. Some like me sat in deep thought, analyzing their physical appearance. I wanted to look back and find the guy who I felt had saved me. But I kept my eyes forward. I was happy. "He said that I'm all right, that I have a nice body. Maybe I'm not dark and ugly after all. Maybe my body and long hair worked." I thought, "Ok, Chara, new mission in life: keep your nice body and long hair, and you will stand out. You won't be average. You will be pretty and accepted. Or at least 'all right.'"

Back to the Library

As I sat in the campus library, I turned from these vivid, formative memories, now realizing why Ken's words had crushed me so much. I had been on a mission since eighth grade to keep all my physical features right in order to be accepted, in order to prove I wasn't dark and ugly. I wasn't going to give up that easily because of Ken's reaction to me. I determined to start all over again on my mission to be pretty. "That's ok," I thought. "My hair will soon grow back, and everything will fall right back into place." I didn't try to see my beauty from within; I didn't know what that even meant. My strategy was simple and very practical: focus on hair growth. "Just grow your long hair back, Chara." Surely, nothing else could possibly go wrong.

CHAPTER 3

THE BEGINNING

Freshman year in college, before I met Ken, I looked in the mirror and saw that several little bumps had appeared on my face, particularly in my forehead area. I called my dad. "Daddy, I have these little bumps appearing on my face. They're like… little… and they're all over my forehead. What should I do? What is this?" My dad has always been my best friend. His words to me were like words from the Bible—always right. "Well, Chara," he said, "you're living on a college campus now, and it could be the fact that you're drinking sodas and stuff. Before you left, we stopped bringing sodas into the house. So try to stop drinking them and see what happens." Just like that, the bumps went away. From that day forward in 1999, I never drank another soda. That's how much I feared anything appearing on my face or messing up my skin.

Having problematic skin was never a thought I even considered as a teenager. I'd never had any acne issues to consider. But in my mind, being a brown girl or a dark-skinned cute girl, meant that physical perfection was a requirement. By this time, the media was portraying all dark-skinned girls with long hair, sexy clothes, and flawless skin.

My father did his best to protect his four little girls from seeing the unrealistic and potentially harmful view of beauty being displayed in the media and throughout the airwaves. The rule in my house, all the way up to the day we left for college, was that we could *not* watch music videos. Not because my dad was overly religious or anything like that; his standard was just not to entertain trash. But guess who would sneak to watch music videos *every* day and knew the words to *every* single song? Me! Guilty as charged. I had no idea what my dad was trying to protect me from. All I knew was that I hated that rule and disobeyed it often. Looking back, I wonder how much different my mind-set would have been if I'd listened to and obeyed my dad. Media definitely had a profound effect on me. I wanted to look like the girls in the videos: long hair, nice body. Who knew I would need to add perfect skin to the list?

What Is This on My Face?

It was the *last* month of college, and graduation was upon me. I had been through the fire with my senior college classes. It wasn't supposed to be like this—stressful and uncomfortable. I'd strategically planned to take one particular professor's courses during my senior year, because he was known as the easiest professor. I thought it was the perfect plan. A few college classmates in my major did the same thing. We'd had him during our freshman year and made the decision then to get the hard professors out of the way and stick with the easiest one for our last year. I'd saved him for three of my senior classes, and I had five classes total. Genius, right? I could not have been more wrong. During the beginning of my senior year, this professor had a heart attack. He survived but had multiple surgeries that caused him to be out the rest of the school year. All I could think when the news was announced was "Your senior year is about to be a living hell." And pure hell it was!

The college dean and others in charge voted to bring in other professors from the top university business departments in the state. I promise you, I threw up almost every night, wondering if I would graduate. The work was grueling. The new professors expected us to be on a level we really weren't on. The presentations for financial reports, formulas, and math problems were so foreign to me that I failed everything the beginning of that year. We all did. So, we banded together as a class and studied our butts off into the wee hours of the morning. We were all scared, each pulling our weight to graduate. On top of that, I was working on my production, and we had to have added rehearsals. Not to mention, I was also a resident's assistant. So I had to be in the lobby area of my dorm at certain hours and couldn't go straight to sleep after long days like everyone else could. "Stressed" was an understatement. In hindsight, I see why my hair fell out. I was stressed, overworked, and giving my body no rest.

Two months before graduation, I remember being on duty, walking into my new dorm room area, and shaking. Apparently, it had become my norm, because I looked up, and this tall, dark, handsome guy was staring at me. I looked away, wondering, "Who is he staring at?" When I glanced back over, he started walking toward me. He wasn't smiling but was looking straight at me as he approached. Frowning, I stared at him. What came out of his mouth shocked me.

"Excuse me, but I have noticed something about you that I can't ignore, and God has instructed me to minister to you." Wait, what? Did he just say, "God said... the Lord said?" I laughed. Not because it sounded weird. As a matter of fact, I was used to biblical language. I was known as the spiritual *chica* on campus by those who knew me. I was the one always encouraging people and putting Bible verses on display in my dorm. So I'm not sure why I laughed.

The guy told me I was displaying symptoms of worry and anxiety, and this was not the will of God. He quoted several familiar Scriptures, and we discussed them. I was adamant that I knew the Scriptures he was referring to, and he was adamant in telling me that I wasn't living them.

I remember him telling me that God had called me to live a life free from worrying about anything. I argued with him: "That's impossible." He went deeper, trying to convince me to really live the Scriptures that I knew. I almost became offended. But by the end of the conversation, I'd admitted he was right and asked him to pray with me. He did and smiled, while encouraging me more.

When he smiled, it hit me: "I'm actually talking to 'the dark-chocolate god.'" This was a very handsome, dark-skinned young man who'd been given this nickname by the females on campus. He was a new student who had come later in the year. His teeth were so white and beautiful—and even more evident when he smiled—highlighting his dark, smooth complexion. He was well-built and often wore shirts showing off his muscular physique.

Later that night, I thought on my conversation with Mr. Tall-Dark-and-Handsome. I still believed that worrying would be impossible for me *not* to do. However, his encouragement made me meditate on some Bible verses more, and I felt a deep conviction to trust the God I had always believed was truly *for* me.

Now with only one month till graduation, I quoted my Scriptures daily and found myself in a more peaceful place. This gentleman's encouragement really did work, and I couldn't wait to tell him. I eventually found him on campus and thanked him. I told him that his conversation had changed me and that I would always remember what he'd taught me. We talked for about forty minutes, and he gave me that beautiful, bright smile. I smiled in return.

That same week, I woke up and noticed I had a bump on my forehead, right in between my brows. I noticed it but didn't really care. There was so much to do. The production, research paper, payments for graduation, finals... My life was moving nonstop toward the looming question "Will I graduate, or not?"

Finally, the verdict was in. I was graduating with honors! When I got the news, I hit the floor in tears. Me? Graduating with honors? I had no words. Of course, I had to tell my new friend "the dark-chocolate god," because my old friend Ken hadn't been around since I'd cut my hair.

Finding my new "spiritual friend" around campus, I hurried toward him to share my news. From a distance, he seemed excited to see me coming and came my way. But when he got closer, he started acting... different. He acted like he didn't want to talk. He cut the conversation short and sort of brushed me off.

I thought, "Is something in my nose?" So I grabbed a mirror from my bag, but before I could finish, I remembered I had that bump on my face. But this was no ordinary bump. It was bigger than the day before and really hard to the touch. I'd been so busy that I'd completely forgotten about it. I hadn't experienced skin problems since that one month of acne my freshmen year. "What is this? Is this a bump? Why is it so hard, and why does it seem way bigger than normal? Is this why Mr. Tall-Dark-and-Handsome cut our conversation short?"

It took a month for the bump to go away, and when it was finally gone, I thought nothing else of it—until I remembered how I was treated by "the dark-chocolate god." I was disappointed. Not necessarily crushed, just shocked at the behavior of this supposed man of God. I didn't really bother to seek his attention again. It was another reminder to me that only perfection equaled acceptance.

Sisterly Love

I wasn't aware that the bump that had appeared on my face the week of graduation was called a nodule—a hard acne lesion, lodged deep within the skin. I thought it was just a bump that took forever to leave. When it finally cleared, I had graduated. Nothing else appeared for about two months. By this time, life for me had begun to change. My twin sister and I had gone separate ways and were living different lives, not seeing each other as much. She'd moved out of the house and started graduate school, while I stayed behind to work. I had mild acne at the time—one or two bumps every now and then but nothing too concerning. I thought it was caused by the makeup I'd been using, so I stopped wearing makeup altogether.

I started living without makeup and surprisingly didn't have too many worries about my face. About six months later, I moved out of my parents' house, and the acne began appearing more often, becoming bigger in size. By this time, my hair had grown back, and I kept it looking healthy to offset what was going on with my face. Still new to experiencing skin issues, I was definitely bothered. But I had high hopes it was just a phase.

One day, my family decided to meet up at a theme park. It would be the first time I'd seen my twin sister in a while. When we saw each other, we hugged and laughed, made jokes about my mom, and laughed some more. We loved messing with her behind her back. When we got alone at some point that day, my sister said, "Hey girl, my face used to look like that right when I started graduate school. I went to the dermatologist, and boom, I was fixed!"

I looked at her in shock. "You mean there's a cure for this?"

"Yeah, girl! You should go."

I went to a dermatologist that same week, and sure enough, just like that, I was fixed. Within one month, my skin cleared. The doctors gave me antibiotics and told me to take them once a day. My skin was back to normal—except each bump left a dark scar. I started wearing makeup again on a consistent basis. I felt pretty. My skin was clear, my body was developing in all the right places, and my hair was long again. You couldn't tell me anything. At twenty-two years old, I was in the prime of my life, discovering my career path, and looking for Mr. Right. During that season of my life, I moved to Savannah, Georgia, for the summer; Michigan for a semester; then back home to Mississippi. I was enjoying life.

While home in Mississippi, I found a job until I could figure out my next move. I was happy. No one knew that I was on acne medication. There was no need to share. None of my friends knew. Besides, I didn't have many friends, and that was okay with me. I dated a couple of guys for short periods, and the only thing they noticed about my skin was that it was a little oily. But that was nothing a little M·A·C or Lancôme couldn't fix. The pills worked wonders. I took those antibiotics every day like clockwork, totally unaware of the *guaranteed* expiration date.

CHAPTER 4

FIXED FOR PERFECTION

"Excuse me, ma'am, but is that a wig?"
"Oh no, this is my real hair."
"Well, it's beautiful."

I got this a lot. No one knew how long I'd waited to be complimented in such a way again. Wigs and weaves were just becoming popular, and many thought the full, thick, bouncy hair on my head was fake. My hair had grown back to its healthy state, and I loved it! I even colored it light brown. Not only was my hair gorgeous again, my skin was flawless now as well! In addition to clearing the acne, the antibiotics seemed to help clear up the dark spots, too. And if that wasn't enough, my body had become the ideal size. I was a size 4, with bangin' hips and a small waist. I'd started getting noticed by random guys I'd meet in all types of settings—church, work, stores, you name it. I was finally measuring up to society's view of beauty, getting attention from the opposite sex and the same sex. Their attention confirmed to me that I was among the best of them. I remember thinking, "If only Ken could see me now." It would've been perfect timing if he did, because, like Beyoncé put it, I was *"feelin' myself."*

Even though I'd grown up in church and my parents were faithful members, by age twenty-three I wasn't attending as often. The church I was raised in was actually quite fun. To this day, it has an awesome children and youth ministry. There was always something to do, and the youth I grew up with were full of personality and adventure.

During my young adult years, I would visit every now and then, since I still lived in the same state. I was at that stage of searching for a mate, a husband to love me for life. I didn't understand why I was single. I made sure to dress in the latest styles and to look exceptionally nice every time I went out. I wanted to meet someone and was open to having a serious relationship. I always dressed in my Sunday best to go to church. *My* Sunday best wasn't the traditional dress or skirt. Nope. I rocked a cute blazer, fitted skinny leg jeans, and four-and-a-half-inch heels. Simple but cute. A nontraditional outfit for a nondenominational church—and I loved it.

I remember church was especially good one Sunday. It was packed, so I wanted to leave right after service was over to beat traffic. As I walked down the stairs, I saw a guy walking out as well. I paid him no extra attention because someone stopped me to talk as I was walking out. It was my home church, so I could never leave without visiting with someone. As I ended my conversation and walked outside, the same guy was now returning from getting something out of his car. I looked up. "Ken? Is that you? Oh my goodness!"

I couldn't believe my eyes. Ken, my friend from college who'd basically dumped our friendship because my hair was no longer lengthy as he'd liked it, was standing right in front of me. Good ol' Ken—the ex-friend who'd said I was "just Chara"—was standing face-to-face with me, in the flesh. I thought to myself, "Pinch me, I *must* be dreaming." But I wasn't. And thank God I wasn't because I… was… *fierce*!

Dark and Lovely

"Chara, is that you? Oh my God, you look so good."

"Well, thank you, Ken. You don't look so bad yourself."

"Wow! It's good to see you, Chara."

"So good to see you too, Ken."

"I'm serious; you look good."

I wanted to turn into Naomi Campbell and walk my imaginary runway! He kept repeating himself, stating that I looked great. He looked good himself. I asked him what he'd been up to, allowing him the chance to update me on his life. He'd graduated a year after me and shared that he'd returned home to live in the same small city he grew up in. He in turn asked me for an update on my life, but as I started talking, he looked up and said, "Hey, okay, well, I gotta go. My fiancée is coming. Good seeing you." I shook my head in shock. He smiled at me and then smiled back at whoever was approaching from behind me. As he backed away toward his car, he shouted out to me to take care, seemingly so his fiancée could hear. But I did not allow him to get off the hook that fast.

"Whoa! Who? Your who?"

"My fiancée. She is walking up behind you now. So I gotta go, okay?"

"Oh no sir, I want to meet her."

I wanted to meet the Barbie that Ken had picked. I just knew she was the picture-perfect supermodel that he'd searched and searched for during our college years. I could hear her footsteps as she came closer. Slowly, I turned, ready to smile and embrace her. I looked past the woman approaching me, searching for a lady with long hair flowing in the wind, but there was no one else behind her. "Surely *she's* not his fiancée?" First of all, she was frowning at me, and I know she saw me smiling at her. Second, based off of my friend's description of the women he wanted back when we were in school, she was definitely not the supermodel type. Her hair was pinned up, and she wasn't wearing any makeup. Her clothes weren't fitted at all, and she wore a long "church" dress. What was most shocking was she didn't even have the perfect skin, nor the biggest butt or the thickest hair. Again, I thought, "*She* is his fiancée?"

How could this be? Did he mature? Did he bump his head?

Was he being forced to marry her? Did he now see that outer appearance didn't equal real beauty? Maybe he did, but I doubted it. I was shocked and confused. Some of my friends said that maybe he fell in love with her personality. My thoughts were, "Please... not *my* ex-friend." Personality was last on his list. As a matter of fact, I remember him saying he could change a female's personality if she was pretty enough.

On the drive home, I couldn't stop thinking about how Ken used to talk so passionately about having the perfect-looking girl and making sure she represented him well by her looks and the way she dressed. Yet he chose *her*. I wasn't hurt, sad, or mad—just confused. Deep down, I truly wanted to believe he regretted not making me his fiancée. I wanted to believe he regretted ending our friendship and got in the car with the current woman in his life upset and angry with himself for missing out. Missing out on what, you ask? Missing out on the new, physically perfect Chara.

Keeping It Real

If I don't keep it real with you, then I won't be helping anybody. So let's really talk about it—and I mean *seriously* talk about it.

During my secret music video watching as a kid, I once saw a girl with skin the color of chocolate walk into a room filled with guys. The guys were minding their own business when one of them looked up and noticed her. He whistled at her. Then, all the other guys noticed her. They too started whistling. She was dressed in a fitted black dress, showing off her perfectly shaped body. Her hair was long and curly. She smiled as they whistled and hovered over her to get her number. A look of pure bliss and satisfaction showed on her face; she'd gotten their attention. She walked the room, gloating and full of herself because she had a pool of men to choose from, and they were begging to be picked.

Totally absorbed in the video, I heard the fumbling of a

key in the door. It was my dad coming in from working late. Since the rule in my house was that we were not supposed to watch music videos, I quickly turned off the TV, ran to my room, and pretended to be asleep. I heard my dad greet my mom, "Hey, honey." And as always, he turned on the light in our room to check on us and make sure we were in bed.

I dodged the bullet of getting caught by my dad that night. But I hadn't dodged an even bigger one. Even my perfect dad—and I do mean perfect—couldn't save me from the images I'd harbored, that now dictated what beauty was for me. The image of the girl with fitted clothing, long hair, perfect skin, and a nice body was what got guys' attention, and in my mind, *that was beauty*.

Movie images, magazines, and even people confirmed this mentality for me. From elementary school to adulthood, society drilled this image into my head. Products were—and still are, I might add—sold to help us be "that girl," the girl who steals the attention of men. Music lyrics confirmed that beauty meant having a flawless image, and certain medical procedures even became popular to help women get the perfect body. This was beauty for me, and getting to a place called Pretty, for me, meant perfection.

So you see, it was important for Ken to see the new, physically perfect Chara. I delighted in the fact that he had a chance to see this dark-skinned girl looking so *chocolicious*. After all, in my mind, I had arrived to that place of Pretty. I had the long hair, beautiful skin, nice butt, perfect waist, and big breasts. I'm just being real about it. I felt I had arrived at real beauty. I patted myself on the back as I played Ken's compliments over and over in my head. I had finally become that vision of beauty I aspired to become. I had believed and conceived society's definition of beauty: being perfect on the outside. I took no thought for my inner condition. After all, I didn't feel broken, I was flawless on the outside and felt good—super good. But to know no other definition of beauty is to know brokenness and lack of fulfillment. I would soon learn this hard truth.

CHAPTER 5

A PRETTY PLACE

"Sir, please, sit down."
"@%^&*#$?∑α8, you can't tell me what to do," the angry third grader said. "You ain't my momma!"
"Stop turning over the desk! Stop throwing things now and sit down!"
"I will hurt you!" The student had failed a couple of grades. He was bigger and stronger than the others in his class. He picked up a chair and threw it at me, then charged at me to stab me with his pencil. Thankfully, I was able to dodge the chair and when he ran towards me, I ran out the room. A strong male teacher was able to stop him before he could hurt me or someone else. It wasn't a pleasant moment.

At lunch, I placed my head down on the desk in frustration. Here I was getting ready to turn twenty-four years old, loving my look and every single thing about it, yet single and hating my job. I was beautiful yet unfulfilled. I was in search of the perfect career and a man. At my job, I was the support teacher in charge of taking the so-called "bad" elementary kids in a separate room to be taught when they couldn't function in the regular classroom. They called it "in-school suspension."

My father believes there's no such a thing as a bad child.

He believes kids are just active or misguided. But he wasn't in that classroom. Those kids were B-A-D! Don't get me wrong; I once agreed with my father. But when that third-grade student decided to throw a desk at me and try to stab me with his pencil, my mind-set changed.

So I sat alongside the kids in the cafeteria, with a small, yellow sticky pad and a pen in front of me. I wrote down my thoughts until I ran out of paper. I asked myself, "What is it that you want to do with your life, and what gifts and talents would you like to use?" After writing in-depth answers to those two questions, I marched into my supervisor's office, announced that I wouldn't be renewing my contract for the upcoming school year, and walked out. I was basically quitting.

I refused to settle and live a mediocre life. Every time I walked into that elementary school building, I felt empty. My patience was quickly running thin with the kids. I knew working with younger children wasn't my calling in life. I've always had a passion for working with teens, and if a teen had thrown a chair at me, my reaction would've been totally different. I might have said, "Hey, let's talk this out. What's going on? What's the problem?" I would have displayed more tolerance and a greater level of understanding—and it never would have progressed to a teen trying to stab me.

That moment with the third grader showed me that I needed to follow my heart and go after what I knew I wanted to do. The question now was, "*How?*" How was I going to go after what I truly wanted? I didn't know. I just knew I couldn't stay there another year. I had one more month to finish with the contract, and I was done.

Telling the Parents

"You did what?" My mom wasn't having it. "If you don't march your butt right back into that office to get your job back, you betta!" In her mind, I had quit and would become homeless.

"Ma, calm down. I will find something. I have time."

"Chara!"

"Ma, it's ok. Something will come through."

At the time I was working at the school, I'd moved back in with my parents, so I didn't really think twice about quitting. To me, it was the perfect time to discover my calling. To my mom, it was a big cause for concern. Daily, she'd drill me on what my next steps should be and spoke of one lady that I should call. "So you want to work with teens, huh? Well, you need to call my friend. She has numerous programs. Call her," urged my mother. But I never did.

The school year ended. I finished my last month and said my goodbyes to my students and the few friends I'd made at the school. With no leads, I was still determined not to renew my contract. I just couldn't. Fear grabbed me, but I continued to look for a job that allowed me to use the gifts and talents I was yearning to use. I prayed and asked God to lead and guide me. I had to trust Him.

Then one Saturday morning, my *life* shifted.

The house phone rang, waking me out of my sleep. "Who in the world still has a house phone?" I thought to myself. My parents weren't home, and I realized it wasn't morning, so I answered the phone.

"Hello?"

"Hi, is this Chara?

"Ummm yes. Who is this?"

"Chara, your mother told me about your desire to work with teenagers."

For some odd reason, I rolled my eyes but stayed open to the conversation. The lady on the other line said she had an emergency. One of her lead facilitators had canceled on her, and she needed someone to go with her to facilitate a program for teens.

"When?" I asked.

"Well, Chara, I know that it's last-minute, but I would need to pick you up within an hour. We will ride to the facility together because you can't get in without me."

"Where?"

What came out of her mouth would show me that God didn't just *hear* my prayers, He had answered them. No one knew what I'd written on my yellow sticky paper but me. I never told my mother; I never shared with anyone. I just listed exactly what I wanted to do, and this call confirmed that God had answered my prayers and that I was on the right track.

"I'm sorry, can you repeat that? Where?" I asked.

Effortlessly

I was headed to a juvenile correctional center—a state prison facility for teen girls—with the lady on the phone. I rushed to get dressed, smiling the entire time and thinking about what was to come. Would a riot break out? Would they listen to me? Could they get along with each other? What would I be allowed to bring? No one knew that on the yellow sheet of paper, I'd written that I really wanted to work with the most challenging teens in the state of Mississippi. I never imagined I would be walking into a facility that housed girls who'd committed crimes. I was amazed and shocked. When the lady arrived, I introduced myself and got in her car. Awkward, I know because I didn't even know her, personally. She was my mom's friend. The one who she kept begging me to call.

On the way to the prison, she introduced herself as Mae Henry. She explained that she would take the lead, and I could watch and assist. She made it clear that she usually never led the groups but only assisted as her lead facilitator took over the program. She was the owner and founder of the program but appeared nervous to take the lead as she described the program to me. You would think I would sit in the car with her and just ride along and only assist when and where needed. But I didn't. I couldn't. When she started to explain that she was still trying to figure out what she would do, I blurted out, "I know you don't really know me, but if you give me about twenty-five to thirty minutes of quietness as you drive, then I can sit here and create a lesson for the girls that can change their lives."

Did I just ask her to be quiet for twenty-five to thirty minutes in her own car? Oh my God? What was I thinking? To my surprise, she responded, "Sure!" She turned the music up and allowed me to work. I asked her to name all the supplies she had in her truck and started my process of thinking and planning. Exactly twenty-two minutes later, I had finished. That life-changing lesson was created. Had I ever done this before? No! But something in me had always wanted to create challenging but fun lessons and workshops for teens that would convey life-altering messages. I announced in excitement, "I got it!" She listened to my idea, the structure of the game I'd planned, and the discussion component to home in on the message. She was intrigued, thrilled, and even relieved. The question in my mind now was, "Will this work?"

We walked toward the tall gates that surrounded the building. Hearing the gates shut behind us reminded me that I was going into a place filled with teens who had committed crimes and wouldn't be leaving anytime soon. Once inside, we could hear the girls laughing and screaming as they prepared to transition to a room where we would be speaking. The guards instructed them to move in an orderly fashion. Mae and I stood in a foyer area waiting for the guards to finish searching our items. As the girls passed by where I was standing, they had no idea I would be their guest speaker. My heart started pounding. They had an air of boldness about them, as if they would stand up and boo me right out of the prison.

After being patted down and retrieving my personal belongings from a basket held by a guard, I looked at my new mentor, the lady from the other end of the phone, the lady who was now trusting me to deliver a powerful message to the teens. I was in utter fear. She had no idea my heart was pounding as fast as it could. I followed her down the hallway. My thoughts started racing. The closer we got to the room, the more I could hear the girls laughing and talking about one another. They scoffed and scolded each other as if guards weren't even in the room. My new mentor got their attention.

"Well, hello, ladies. We have a treat for you today—a guest speaker!" She was announcing me as soon as we walked in. I had to start talking to myself: "Calm down, Chara. Be you. Be confident. They will follow your lead, so lead them. You got this. I know you haven't done this before, but this is what you do—do it!" By nature, I knew my gifts and talents, but had never really put them into action, and here was my chance. "Chara, *lead*. They need what you have." I found myself face-to-face with hard stares. The teenage girls looked like women who'd been to hell and back but acted like third graders in need of attention.

"Hello ladies. Let's get started!" I showed them a small teddy bear and asked them to pretend it was a microphone. "We're going to have a real discussion after we play a game. If you are holding the teddy bear, you have the floor. If not, you should be listening to the person who is." We played the fun game, and then it was time for the discussion. I asked a simple question, "Who wants the bear first?"

Exactly one hour later, as we walked out of the room to leave the prison, the girls were shouting statements and questions all at the same time: "When are you guys coming back?" "Come back tomorrow." "Thank you!" "We enjoyed you!" "Hey, bring food next time!" The program was a complete success! And in that moment, I was thrilled—and fulfilled.

My new mentor hired me before we even left the building. She was impressed and expressed to me that I had done a wonderful job. In fact, she was so impressed that she made me a promise. "Chara, you should be doing this for a living. I can't pay you much, but I will find you a program that can pay you more than I can." I thought she was just talking and didn't really expect her to keep her promise. Besides, I was still on cloud nine from doing something I absolutely loved. She didn't know this was my first time presenting, my first time using my gifts in this way. It was a real success, the beginning of a career that would bring my world to complete happiness. Going to the prison was so rewarding. I went every other weekend, eventually becoming a guest speaker at her other locations. She became someone I truly looked up to—and still look up to today. At that time, I didn't think life could get any better, but because of her, it did!

I started traveling to the female prison alone and became a familiar guest to the staff. On one occasion, I even planned an outdoor retreat for the teen inmates. It was the first of its kind—something really different for the girls to attend. That, too, was a success. I was eventually contracted to go to a male juvenile prison. My summer was busy and filled with speaking engagements from Mae Henry personally and from all her other programs. I traveled far and wide, and I loved every bit of it.

Close to the end of the summer, Mae Henry—who is now *Dr.* Mae Henry—called me and kept her promise, even though I had already forgotten it. But she did exactly what she'd said. She'd found me a well-paying job. Not just any job but a job that would allow me to travel and speak to at-risk teens in the rural areas of Mississippi schools and communities. My job was to develop creative content and use evidence-based curricula that promoted abstinence and character education. The job would pay me well, with insurance. This would be my first real full-time job—my *main* job—and I was so happy.

When I went in for the interview, I was asked to present a lesson to the employees who were supposed to be role-playing teens. The goal was to see how I would handle an unruly class. They went a bit over the top, behaving more like toddlers than teens, but I was still able to steal the show. I'd researched the area of teens they served and created a game that would eventually become one I taught to other staff members. The director was impressed. She said she'd originally wanted to hire someone from the area, but I was too good to pass up. I later found out that my mentor told her she wouldn't find anyone better.

After my presentation, I was hired on the spot, and I couldn't wait to tell my mentor. She'd had a profound impact on me. Her one phone call to me on a Saturday morning had prepared me in a way I didn't know I would soon need. Years later, she told me that her husband had made her call me. She was going to go to the prison alone, to wing it. I'm so glad she didn't.

Life was good again—so good. I loved my look and my job. I was happy. Talk about living in my "pretty" place.

Next up: find a man. Who wouldn't want me now? I'd been on a mission for years to live in that "pretty" place where I was now living. I expected life to only get better. But what would happen to me next would be the unthinkable—the unexpected and the unacceptable. I was aware that seasons change in one's life, but I never knew a season could totally change for the worse so quickly.

CHAPTER 6

WAKE ME, I'M DREAMING!

"Is he flirting with me?" I thought. I was intrigued. This older, single principal was definitely my type. Still, I wasn't too certain about his character, and I wasn't sure he was really single, so I never really took him seriously. He kept his personal life private. Nevertheless, I enjoyed the attention he gave me and looked forwarded to the speaking engagements at his school every other week.

In my new job, I was traveling to rural and urban schools during the week and juvenile prisons on the weekend to present innovative content *my way*. I was really good at it. Creative ideas would just come to me, and I loved it. I thanked God He opened the door for me to do exactly what I wanted.

August was my first week of class in a new school. I would drive from my new apartment, in my new car, to present to hundreds of teens. Going from class to class, I was speaking to different groups of teens all day. I felt beautiful. Skin glowing and hair still long and beautiful, I picked out the perfect outfits to complement my body size. I considered myself a stylish speaker. I was cute and content. By October, students and teachers alike looked forward to my visits. I became a popular guest teacher. An attractive, single black female, walking into a school, vibrant and full of life. It wasn't a surprise that I'd befriended all the male principals. I was friends with some of the female principals as well. Outgoing and easy to get along with—that's just who I was.

"Hmmm… is my future husband a principal?" I wondered. I was now on a mission to find a man. After all, my career was in place. All that was left was to find the perfect man.

Lumps or Bumps

I woke up each morning, took my acne pills as usual, and got ready for my day. But one day I woke up, and something had changed. "What is this on my face?" I'd been taking the acne medication just as prescribed for a little over two years straight, never missing a single day. So what was this? Whatever it was brought all my happiness and contentment to a screeching halt.

I was having a breakout. Two bumps were forming on my face that looked more like lumps than regular acne blemishes. My face looked swollen. Still, I knew what they were forming into. They took the same form as during my last days in college when I ran into Mr. Chocolate. I didn't want to go teach on that day, but I had to and of all the days… the school principal I really liked had finally asked me to go out to dinner after school. He knew it was my day on campus and sent me an email. I was so afraid that I would run into him. I messaged back sharing that I had a doctor's appointment on the other side of town and needed to leave right after school. I had booked it that morning and I really couldn't miss the dermatologist appointment, especially after what I'd just awakened to that morning. Even if I didn't make an appointment, I wasn't going out with him with such an unusual breakout on my face.

The appointment was set, and I went to see the same doctor who had given me the first batch of acne medicine. The medications I was taking weren't working as well as before, so he switched them and started me on new treatments. I felt things would return to normal soon, and the new pills would work just as the old ones had once I picked up the prescription. The doctor didn't give me any indication or warning that my body could become resistant to the medications. I simply expected them to work. I started taking the medications, and sure enough, the two lumps went down. However, smaller bumps started to appear. They weren't as inflamed, so I was still comfortable with going to schools and seeing people. Besides, it wasn't a big deal; my new pills would take care of it—or so I thought.

Four weeks later, I was creating a new lesson, one I was excited to teach. I jumped up that morning to look at my face. "How? What? Why?" was all I could think. The small bumps from the day before were now bigger—bigger than normal. They'd started to form into huge, hard lumps. I didn't understand. Confused and at a loss, I wanted to cry. I wanted to take more pills, as if something magical would happen. Instead, I called the doctor and requested a higher dosage of the medications. I wore extra makeup that day, in hopes of covering the lumps and keeping the teens from noticing them. After all, I still had to go to work. The teens and teachers depended on me.

When I went in to work that day, I walked into the room of teenagers, and one of the teens said to another, "Ugh, she has bad acne."

The other teen replied, "She's still pretty, though."

Pretty Please

After work, I headed straight to the pharmacy to pick up the higher dosage of medication I'd requested. I cancelled the rest of my classes that week and waited for my skin to heal. I pushed each speaking engagement to the following week because surely by then my skin would be healed. Right? That next week, not only were the lumps still there but more bumps had appeared on my face.

I pretended the condition of my skin didn't bother me and continued to go to work, teaching as usual. Oh, but it did. The breakouts continued to happen. When they did, I'd go straight to the class I was teaching that day, skipping my normal visits to see my principal friend and any other male adults I'd befriended.

At first, the bumps appeared as regular acne, and I was able to go to the school, teach my lessons, and leave. Honestly, I just looked like some of the teens going through puberty. But, as the days went by, a couple of the bumps appeared to be abnormal. They became seriously inflamed, turning into something I'd never seen before. They were large and blistered. My face looked like it was covered in boils, surrounded by small patches of acne. It was extremely painful, but I couldn't even cry because I was in such disbelief at what I was seeing when I'd looked in the mirror. The bumps were harder than normal, and I could barely wash my face because of the pain. Wearing makeup was pointless. I needed a new dermatologist, pronto! I immediately called and cancelled my school schedule for two weeks, letting the schools know that I'd had what I believed was an allergic reaction and was headed to the hospital.

I didn't go to the hospital, but surely this was a reaction to the medications, I thought; it was too extreme. My face was disfigured and totally abnormal in appearance. I began searching for an African American female doctor in the state of Mississippi. It didn't matter how much she cost. I was willing to break the bank. What was happening to my face was out of control and unacceptable. Something had to give—and I was willing to give everything.

Help Me

I found her, an African American female dermatologist. At the time, she was the only black female dermatologist available to see. I was so hopeful and happy to see her. I'd imagined her walking up to me with a plan of action, along with sympathy and a heart full of compassion. I jumped at the first available appointment.

I walked into the dermatologist's office, feeling like a monster. In my opinion, I looked like one, too. I kept my head down the entire time I was there. The nurse walked me back after checking my vitals, and she could tell I was ashamed to look up at her. Still, she treated me kindly. She went out of her way to show me that I was not a monster, that everything would be okay. She placed me in a room and told me the doctor would see me shortly.

While waiting for the doctor, I looked in a mirror in front of me, and for first time, I felt like crying. I was out of my state of disbelief, and my emotions broke free. Sitting right there in that doctor's office, gazing into a mirror, I burst into tears. I didn't even recognize myself. I sat there and I cried and cried. My appearance had changed so suddenly that I hadn't even processed how I looked. I looked ugly, and I felt ugly. I felt such hopelessness.

Everything was perfect just weeks before. After years of trying, I'd finally made it to a place called "pretty" and enjoyed every moment of it. I was confident and comfortable in my beautiful chocolate skin, with my ideal figure. I finally believed *I* could be someone's trophy wife. Now, here I was sitting in a doctor's office, wishing I could return to the look I had when I was in the third grade, or even the look I had in eighth grade when I was booed on the bus. Nothing was wrong with me back then—absolutely nothing! If only I could've appreciated my looks and my life then.

I even wished I could return to my college days and tell Ken, "Short hair, don't care," because, truly, nothing was wrong with me. I thought to myself, "Why couldn't I have embraced my beauty, my natural beauty, back before anything took place with my skin?" Again, nothing was wrong with me then. But at this particular moment, as I sat waiting for the doctor, something actually was wrong with me. My face was disfigured.

And then things got worse for me. I attribute some of the extreme self-consciousness, insecurities, and mental pain that would come in the days ahead to my visit with the dermatologist—the one I'd prayed to see. Her response to me wasn't anything like I'd imagined. I walked in needing her more than she knew. I expected to leave with some type of comfort, some type of peace. I had questions and concerns. I was crying out, waiting for her arrival, thinking, "Tell me everything will be ok, Doc. I'm confused. This is new. Why is this happening? Tell me that you see me, that you've got me and will walk through this with me as my new doctor. Tell me that you've seen this before, and you'll fix me. Give me hope, help me see tomorrow better than today."

Instead of receiving what I longed for, I left her office crying, scarred, bruised, and more fearful than when I came. I felt helpless and mad all at the same time. I wanted to tear that office up, her included. I told her nurse I was going to write a complaint to the American Academy of Dermatology Association about the African American doctor that I thought would help me but instead hurt and crushed me more. The nurse comforted me and encouraged me to do so.

CHAPTER 7

MY NEW NORMAL

Before I can describe to you how the dermatologist negatively impacted my life in that one visit, I want to first tell you about a lady who opened my eyes to *how* and *why* that day changed me forever. I had not known how much my heart was affected until I met this lady, Susie. One day we sat down for lunch, and she shared with me that she and her sixteen-year-old son had been diagnosed with the AIDS virus.

According to the Centers for Disease Control, people are diagnosed with AIDS if their CD4 cell count (white blood cells that fight off infection) is lower than 200 or if they have developed certain opportunistic illnesses. The lower the count, the greater the damage HIV (human immunodeficiency virus) has done to the immune system, and the body cannot fight off infections. HIV is the virus that causes AIDS (acquired immunodeficiency syndrome). There is no cure. However, with proper adherence to HIV treatments, the virus can be controlled, and a person can live a long and healthy life. (CDC, 2019).[4]

My first question (in my head, of course) was, "Why are you telling me this?" My second question was, "How did you contract HIV?" Susie was one of my community volunteers in the rural area. I was a great networker for the company, and I loved meeting people before my skin condition worsened. I was always in someone's face. Always! She and I talked all the time.

When my face started to break out, I would still go see her and help her out with our events, even when I wanted to cancel.

Now, she was telling me about her diagnosis during our lunch, just before one of our big events. We were working associates, not best friends. How did she know I would keep her information confidential? How did she know I wouldn't slip up and accidentally mention it when I taught on HIV/AIDS during our classes? She shared that her first husband cheated on her with a man and was living on the *down-low* ("down-low"— a term meaning he was married but secretly having sexual relationships with men), until he was hospitalized. On his deathbed he confessed and told her to get tested for HIV and to take their son to get tested. My heart broke for her. I grabbed her hand, apologizing as if I'd given her the virus. She smiled and finally answered the question I hadn't asked aloud.

She told me she'd been watching me and recalled a time I'd taught on HIV/AIDS. She recalled how my focus was on helping my audience *understand* the disease and learn to treat *any* infected individual with the utmost respect, regardless of their status. She said that as an AIDS educator herself, she'd listened to hundreds of lectures by people teaching on the disease, but many never catered their messages toward loving and respecting the individual as I did during my lectures. Then she asked me a question I'd never thought twice about until that moment, "Why, Chara—why are you so passionate about individuals living with HIV/AIDS?" All I could do was think about the first day I entered the office of that dermatologist.

What Really Happened

I sat in her office crying, awaiting her arrival, waiting for her to help me and give me answers. My back was to the door and a mirror was facing me as I sat on the medical examination seat, plus I was holding a mirror I'd gotten from the counter. The door opened, and my heart jumped. She, the black dermatologist, called my name. Hesitating, I turned around to face her.

The woman was gorgeous. She had long, light brown hair that perfectly matched her light brown complexion. She appeared to be in her late fifties, but her flawless skin said otherwise. She rocked red pumps with a black dress underneath her white physician's coat. I smiled, happy to see (I hoped) my last dermatologist. For some reason, the thought of having her as my doctor gave me comfort and hope that she'd not only understand me but also my pain.

As I smiled, she looked back at me in shock and frowned. All hope left with one look. She did a double take. I thought to myself, "Yes, it is as bad as it seems." She exclaimed, "Ugh! Oh my God. Gross! Look at you. You have lesions all over your face!" She put gloves on, seeming afraid to touch my face. I thought, "Okay, wait, Doc. I know you're shocked, but isn't this what you see often? Isn't this what you went to school for?" Still frowning, she tapped my face as if I were some kind of science experiment, never placing her hands directly on the lesions. "Gross," she said, as she used one finger to move my chin from side to side and took a closer look. She acted as if I had a contagious disease. Discomfort, tension, and even confusion filled the room, but I forced myself to speak.

"Ummm... Doc... that's why I'm here. I was hoping you could help me. I don't know what to do. I don't know why this has happened to me and so suddenly. The pills I was taking stopped working, and I need—"

"What pills?" When I told her, she said, "Okay, I will prescribe you more, just in a higher dosage," and swiftly left the room. She clearly didn't even want to be in the same room with me and gave me no chance to ask her *any* questions.

I sat in disbelief, completely dumbfounded. My mind started racing. I thought, "First, wait... I just told you the pills I was taking no longer worked for me. They actually appear to have made things worse." Mind you, before recognizing the pills had stopped working, I would take them faithfully. So I was certain the medication had stopped working. "Secondly, I have questions. What's happening to me? What did I do to cause this, and how can I stop it? And Doc… are you coming back?" Seventeen minutes later, I was still sitting in the office, wondering if she'd return. By that time, the shock had worn off, and I wanted answers—along with an apology. She hadn't even wanted me to shake her hand. My thoughts turned into inner screams. I was furious at the way she'd treated me. "YOU ARE MY DOCTOR! TREAT ME WITH RESPECT!" By the time I walked out of the room, my emotions had hit me all at once. They took over, and the sweet nurse became my target.

I started crying and hyperventilating. The nurse took my hand, pulled me back into the room, and kept saying, "Calm down, calm down, you're okay, calm down." When I finally did calm down, I told her I'd never felt so disrespected and hurt before in all my life. I told her just how rude the doctor had been to me and how unacceptable it was for her to treat me the way she did. The nurse was so comforting. But what was most confusing was that she seemed to want me to report the doctor. She kept saying things like, "You really should" and "Yes, that's a good move to make," encouraging me to report what had taken place. I didn't understand it until we walked out of the room and I witnessed how the doctor treated her staff. It wasn't just me she behaved this way with. She was rude to everyone. But her rudeness toward me was now embedded in me. I became even more ashamed of how I looked, and I automatically thought others saw me the same as she did—as contagious and untouchable.

HIV patients are often discriminated against too, even by doctors. You'd think medical professionals would be educated enough about how the disease is contracted and treat everyone equally, but that's not always the case. HIV/AIDS patients are also often ostracized by family members, close friends, and the public if their disease is made known. For this reason, many keep their diagnoses private. I don't mean to overly compare the two conditions, but I do think I became more compassionate toward the ostracized and the stigmatized because of my own experience. When people looked at me, I felt judged and denied. The doctor's reaction was my first experience with feeling that way, and it caused me to put up an internal wall to protect myself from ever feeling that form of rejection again. The only problem was, I couldn't keep my condition private. It was on display for the world to see; it was on my face.

My skin had gotten out of hand. Inflamed boils were on my face day after day and lasted for weeks. I cancelled many days of work, waiting for my face to heal. The medicine no longer worked, and I was desperate, confused, and sad. My job became extremely hard to deal with, because I used my face for a living. How could I travel from school to school teaching about STDs when I looked like I had all of them and then some?

I stopped going to work. I only went when I didn't have what the dermatologist called "lesions" on my face. I took pictures out of disbelief. I still couldn't believe something was growing on my face. When I woke up in the morning, either the two to three lesions were bigger, or another had started to appear, and I would be devastated yet again. But I couldn't give up my fight to get help. That same week, I contacted several other doctors to try to make an appointment. However, this time I wasn't picky. I just wanted a skilled dermatologist, no matter the ethnicity.

Hide, Chara

Dressing down became my norm. I had over ten different baseball caps. If I had lesions or regular acne and had to leave my house, I wore a baseball cap. I hated getting attention from guys from a distance, only to see them react to my face when they came closer. So, to prevent the emotional toll their shock inflicted on me, I wore baseball caps. As a size 4 with a slim waist, I forgot that my body was an attention-getter. I started dressing in baggy joggers. My work wardrobe changed as well.

I wasn't there often, so when I went, I had to make it memorable; that way, if headquarters ever got wind of the days I wasn't coming, they'd only hear about the impact I was making with the students. I still loved what I did, but I was so distracted by what was happening with my face that I found it hard to do my job. I'd made it a routine to go to my classes, teach, and run to my car.

One day, I didn't have much inflammation, but I had at least one boil-like bump on my face, as well as other small acne blemishes. I had to get to the school. It'd been a full month since I last taught. While I was at the school, preparing to teach and leave, the principal I liked came to find me. I saw him from a distance. "Oh no," I thought to myself, "the principal is coming my way… oh no, oh no, oh no… run, Chara, run!" I tried to hide, run, and even duck.

"There you are! I've been looking for you. I've been asking about you. You forgot about me, huh?" He cornered me and grabbed my hand. "Come in my office."

I took a deep breath, "Forget about your face, Chara. Just be cool. At least it's not that inflamed. Be cool." I was nervous. I just knew he'd reject me when he noticed my face. It would be the first time I'd really had a conversation with a male in my new normal. I thought he'd finally make eye contact with me and say, "Ugh, that's ok… leave my office," like others who'd seen my face in that condition. But he didn't.

He did, however, remind me of just how superficial this world could be, and it caused me to latch on even tighter to the world's definition of beauty as I battled to rid myself of the skin condition. He stared at my body, looked me up and down, and his voice tone changed, "Can I be honest with you?"

Knowing where he was going, I interrupted with "Did you just get married?" I noticed he had wedding pictures up in his office. I didn't know he was married. He never wore his ring, and he acted like he was single. He ignored my question and continued to express his feelings, with no shame.

"Da$% girl, you're fine! I mean, turn around." He really wanted me to turn around. "Turn around! Your body is perfect. It's just perfect. I mean, how you come in here and teach abstinence and not think about getting it on? I can tell you the things I can do to you. Listen, let's get together… Friday night. I can tell my lady that I'm at a work conference."

I smiled, looked at him, and told him to have a great day. I guess he was shocked that I walked out of his office, because he rushed out to try to make sure I wouldn't report him or tell anyone. Even though his comments were rude and disrespectful, I honestly was shocked I was still liked, even though it wasn't for the right reasons.

Back in college, everything had to be perfect. But as an adult, I was learning that as long as my body was perfect, some things could be ignored. This beauty thing was getting quite tricky with age. However, deep down, I still felt things would've been different if my skin was really inflamed that day.

My quest for perfection continued. I just had to prevent the inflammation from returning. I needed to get back to a place called "pretty," or I wouldn't ever be liked again. I felt as if I were losing ground. I was moving further and further from society's definition of pretty, as lesions continued to appear on my face. I thought to myself, "Lord, I've got to get to a better place. You gotta heal me. I'm your child. I'm supposed to be beautiful. If I get those lesions on my face again, then I won't make it. It's not normal. It's not supposed to be my norm. Please don't let the lesions return."

CHAPTER 8

And It Starts... The Battle

On the days that boils covered my face, I skipped work. I refused to go anywhere. My motto was "No one can ever see me with lesions—not even my family." Most of my weeks were spent in and out of different dermatologists' offices, trying to figure out which doctor really knew what he or she was talking about. I took any information the doctors gave me seriously. I began using Google to research what was happening to me and discovered I had developed nodulocystic acne. "What is that?" I thought. "And what's causing it?"

After internet-searching the ailment, I learned that it consists of large, firm lumps under the skin called nodules and deep, fluid-filled, painful cysts. Though it starts like regular acne, nodulocystic acne progresses into a more severe state. It also might be genetic, and there's nothing environmental that specifically causes it. No doctor, at that particular time, could tell me a cause. They could only tell me *what* was happening, and that was extremely frustrating, because if I didn't know what was causing it, how could I stop it?

I stayed home a lot. I learned the pattern of my skin, knowing how the breakouts would progress, and arranged my work schedule accordingly. For example, if my acne became inflamed on a Sunday, I would schedule to teach on a Monday or

Tuesday, before the inflammation reached its highest point, and then would return three weeks later. For six months straight, this routine continued, with me cancelling lessons and setting up my schedule around the times my skin wasn't inflamed. I would get full pay working only twice a month, and no one at headquarters really knew. But I knew going to the schools "sick" was not an option. That's how I labeled my skin condition—as me being "sick."

While home, I felt lazy and hated being cooped up; it wasn't what I was used to. One day I decided to compile all the games, activities, and lessons I had created, along with all the new lessons I would have taught if my skin were healed. I compiled them into something like a book or a curriculum. Working on this took my mind off my face and what I looked like; after all, looking in the mirror had become extremely difficult. So while home, I created.

It was a good distraction and took three months to finish. I sent it to an old friend who I knew loved working with youth. Her feedback gave me a boost because she was a tough critic. From there, I decided to include artwork with my curriculum. I mean, why not? I had plenty of time on my hands since it took the nodules on my face weeks to heal. Next step: market my curriculum and send it to a youth organization for purchase. My plan was to try to get paid extra money while hiding at home until I was "fixed."

A month passed, and I received a phone call. I had sent the curriculum off, never really thinking any organization would respond. But one did—and not only did they want to purchase my curriculum, but they wanted to pay me to teach it. So they set up a meeting with me. The organization sponsored a program specifically for youth whose parents were incarcerated. I couldn't believe it. How could I not take this meeting?

I prayed really hard, asking God to heal my face for the day of the meeting. "God, I don't need to be distracted. Please, Jesus, allow these pills to work." By that time, I was taking pills from another dermatologist. "Please, Jesus, do what you do." On the day of the meeting, I had acne—no nodules but a few small cysts. When I arrived, the lighting in the room was very dim. I was thrilled about that. I had become very conscious of how much light was in a room when I entered. A room filled with bright lights meant people would clearly see my face, and that made me super self-conscious. A darker or dimmer room made me feel better.

In the room sat a very professional-looking young man and two other women. The director made her presence known. She wore a nice suit and facilitated the meeting with authority. As a part of the interview, she asked me to role-play scenarios that could occur while at the school. I acted these mock situations out with the young man. He was in a leadership position, ready to take the program into an alternative school, and the director wanted to see if my curriculum could be a good fit. When I say I could have received an Oscar for that performance, I'm not exaggerating. The population for the alternative school in which she wanted to place my curriculum was all too familiar; I was still going to the prison to work with juvenile females at times, so I knew all about what could happen.

I was again hired on the spot. The goal was to use my curriculum in the alternative school. I was assigned to all the girls, and the male employee that I role-played so well with would be over the boys. Also, I could still keep my main job because the schedule was perfect. I was overjoyed and super excited. I drove back home with ideas racing through my head, ready to take the program to the next level.

The girls at the alternative school were middle school students still classified as elementary students. They were fourteen and fifteen years of age and had never moved past the fourth grade. The school was built to help them academically, along with merging in holistic community programming.

Elated as I arrived home, I went straight to my bedroom and grabbed my computer to email my friend the good news. I sat down on the bed and looked up, only to see my reflection in the mirror. I had forgotten about my skin condition. My excitement immediately turned into fear. How, just how, could I face a crowd of students, knowing that my skin wasn't healed yet? The joy turned into fear, and the fear turned into sadness. I shut my computer down, wiped off the makeup that covered my face, jumped into bed, and cried myself to sleep. I never even sent my friend the email. For the first time, I questioned if God would really fix me.

Fix It, Jesus

The male employee and I had talked over the phone and in person about the plans that were to happen the first day at the new alternative school. His name was Patricks. "Yes, Patrick with an *s*," he would always say. He would become an essential part of my life, and our friendship would develop into a brother-sister relationship. But at this point, I didn't know him at all.

We were to meet up at the school and prepare for the first day of programming. It was my day to be introduced to all the staff and students and to get to know Patricks more. This was the first day I would make an impression. I wish I could tell you that my face was clear, but it wasn't, and I felt very insecure. I was wearing a fly dress, stilettos, and jewelry, even though I hated dressing up when my face broke out. I cried the entire forty-minute drive to the school. I felt that dressing up drew attention to me, and I hated receiving attention from afar, only to disappoint up close.

I used to desire attention from afar, up close, up top, and behind when I was physically "perfect." But all that had changed. I didn't want anyone to notice me in any way, because I was far from physical perfection. I wanted to hide in the crowds. I wanted to be in the back, instead of the forefront. I didn't want any attention at all. So when I got out of the car and walked to the door of the school in my dress and heels, I halted. I refused to walk in. I just couldn't. My mind started racing, and all I could think of was how everyone's first impression of me would be seeing a cute girl with a face full of inflamed acne. So I turned from the door to leave. I felt I couldn't do it—at least not until my skin had healed. But as I walked to the car, Patricks pulled up.

"Chara, hey! Where are you going?" he yelled from his beat-up, little white car that he paradoxically seemed extremely proud of. He jumped out and quickly noticed something was wrong. I was pacing, frowning, and nervous to say how I really felt. I questioned if I should tell him my fears or if I should say anything at all. Suddenly I belted out, "Patricks, I can't do this!"

"What? Do what? What do you mean? You don't want to do the program?"

I screamed, "I do, but not like this…"

"Not like what? Chara, what are you talking about?"

Again, right in that moment, I questioned if I should tell Patricks about my fear of walking into the building to be introduced to everybody with cysts on my face. I questioned whether I should tell him that I didn't want to be seen and didn't want to be judged, or how I feared the comments from teachers and students and dreaded that they might treat me as if I were contagious. Would I sound crazy if I told him this? "Am I going crazy?" I had so many thoughts going through my head. I felt ugly and unattractive. I felt devalued and unliked—not just by others but by *me*. I paced and paced.

Finally, Patricks broke the silence. He said carefully and calmly, "Chara, I know you don't know me, but please tell me what's going on in your head." He knew something was wrong; not even knowing me, he knew that I wasn't myself.

I inhaled and exhaled. "Okay… okay… my face… It's my face. Look at it! I just can't, I just can't!"

Patricks looked up at me and grabbed my shoulders. He talked as if he understood me. "Oh, but you can. It doesn't matter how you look. You are here to help so many young girls. You have a gift, Chara. We all saw that when you entered our office. This is just a distraction, stopping you from helping others. I get it. You want clear skin, and okay, this can happen. But right now, in this moment, your courage needs to happen for these teens. They need you. Now, deep breath!"

You would think a speech like that would have motivated me to get moving, drop my fears and insecurities, and start my walk through the double doors of that school. But it didn't. In fact, his advice went in one ear and right out the other. "Okay... okay... okay... wait... I'll tell you what. I can do this, but—and this may sound crazy—let me go home to change clothes."

"Wait, what? But Chara, you look great! Very professional."

I insisted. "Patricks, I just need to dress down, and I can come back here comfortable and be me. Let me get out of this dress, and I can come right back here and be ready for the day. I promise. I just need to change clothes."

"Well, how far do you stay from here?"

"Umm, about fifteen minutes, maybe twenty minutes max," I lied, knowing I really had a forty-five-minute drive.

I felt lost and trapped in my mind. It was as if I couldn't calm myself down and let go of how I looked. My mental battle had become extremely disturbing and uncontrollable. It was what caused me to get in my car and drive all the way home to change clothes. I constantly looked in the mirror in disbelief as I drove. I was hoping my outcome would suddenly change and I would look different, but it didn't and I didn't. This was my reality, but it was hard to accept. Changing clothes and dressing down somehow comforted me and fed into my illusion that no one paid attention to me when I dressed that way.

Opening up to Patricks was my first time talking to someone about how the breakouts affected me and the first time I'd noticed just how deeply insecure and self-conscious I was about my imperfections. It was also the first time I saw the psychological effects that body image dissatisfaction had on me. My own self-image was probably worse than how others actually saw me; after all, I'd known perfection before this, and I always

57

judged myself against that standard. My emotions and thoughts ran my life, and rational thinking escaped me whenever I felt the need to hide or run because of my face.

Trying to get out of my own way, I drove back to the school kind of embarrassed over how I'd acted about my face. I walked right through those double doors in jeans and a blazer —no dress—and went upstairs to the new office I'd be sharing with Patricks. "Welcome back," he said, never mentioning how irrationally I'd acted earlier by leaving the building right before a session to go home and put on jeans. He was focused, and he wanted, in some way, to show me that that's how I was supposed to be—focused. I was introduced to the administrative team and to the students. The mental battle continued. I felt like I could hear their thoughts: "Wow, pretty girl, but what's up with her skin?"

Every second of the day, I wondered what others thought of me and how I looked. In the midst of one of the greatest opportunities of my life, flaws and imperfections ruled my mind, which, in turn, ruled my world. Getting a grip on my mental state would become my biggest battle, even beyond the physical one. But it would be far from the last.

CHAPTER 9

MIRACLE DRUG

"Excuse me, Ms. Chara. Can I talk to you?" said the older, sweet lady who taught computers at the alternative school. "Can we go inside my classroom? My students are away." I had no idea what she wanted to discuss with me. Patricks talked with her often, but this would be my very first conversation with anyone at the school. Since Patricks was prone to holding long conversations with her, I thought perhaps she was going to discuss him with me. People always tried to put us together. They figured we'd be the perfect fit since we worked together and had similar passions. I was preparing myself to give her the "we're just friends" speech. Instead, she pulled me into the room to discuss the unthinkable.

She spoke in a soft voice, seemingly with trepidation, "I know that what I am about to say may cause you pain, because no one understands the emotional impact that you may be facing, but I need to tell you the truth." She took a breath and said, "Dearest, you don't have to walk around looking like that. You can get help." Silence filled the air. I stared at her in disbelief, and she looked at me, waiting for a response.

I knew she wasn't trying to be rude, but she didn't know me or my story. She didn't know all I was doing and had done to get help for my skin. Did she really think I *wanted* to look like I was looking? Did she think I *wanted* lesions on my face?

I thought I was doing good not to have thought about it that day. But she brought it back to my mind, and my emotions took over. I smiled at her, as tears started streaming down my face. I tried to speak, but the tears wouldn't stop. She started to apologize and tried comforting me. She reached out to try to hug me, but I backed away to grab my things and tried to rush out the door. She called out, "No, not yet!" reminding me that students as well as teachers were in the hallway. I just wanted to get to my car, but I didn't want others to see me crying. So I stayed a little bit longer, waiting for the hallway to clear. I needed to be alone. I wouldn't even look at her. I kept trying to stop myself from crying.

Despite my obvious meltdown, she continued to talk to me as if she'd gone through what I was experiencing, but she hadn't. She only *knew of* a loved one who had, and she felt it gave her some insight into my world. I get it now—the loved one was her daughter—but I didn't care at the time. I just wanted her to stop talking to me. But she didn't stop. "I know that what I am saying to you is causing many emotions to surface," she said. "I have been holding this in for so long and have wanted to tell you this. Please listen."

She told me about a drug that had just come on the market and that many dermatologists were using in other states, but mostly not in the state of Mississippi. She explained that I needed to find a doctor who would be willing to try that medication on me and wrote down the name of it. Wiping my eyes and trying to regain composure, I took the information, thanked her, and went to my car, where I cried even more.

I thought about what she said to me and was confused as to how I should feel. I didn't know if I should feel helped or harmed. I saved the name of the medication in my phone to show my doctor. The computer teacher had called it "the miracle drug" for short, and I wrote that down too.

It was now time for me to get out of the car and go back to work. I looked in the mirror, wiped my face, and placed makeup back over the lesions. I hated walking into the school with cysts and lesions on my face. I had been hoping others didn't see me as I saw myself, but that day confirmed that I didn't look good. I felt broken, ugly, and useless, and my mind couldn't convince me otherwise.

I rushed to make an appointment with my doctor, and when I got there, I blurted out, "Doc, have you heard of this miracle drug?" To my surprise, he said yes. I was shocked that, despite all the dermatology visits I'd had, no one had offered me the miracle drug. I wanted to know why. "So you mean there is a drug that can cure what I'm going through, and I'm not on it? What's up with that?" I was excited and mad at the same time, and my doctor could feel my energy.

I saw this as a sign from God—better yet, an answer from God. I'd waited for this moment, and I wanted to be sure I received the blessing I'd been praying for. I had been crying out to God night after night, confused as to why I was going through this when the God I knew to be real was and *is* a healer. So, for me, this moment, this revelation, this miracle drug, was God's answer to me.

However, my doctor didn't seem as excited to tell me about it as I was to hear about it. Just as he felt my energy, I felt his. I insisted he tell me the reason for his lack of enthusiasm. His head hung low, and his speech was soft. He looked at me seriously, "Chara, I know they have deemed this a 'miracle drug,' but it's dangerous, and it's a serious drug. It's basically still in its exploration stage. The FDA has just issued an alert for this drug and all its generics, advising doctors to monitor patients for suicidal thoughts or actions. You must sign an agreement, promising that you will see a psychologist and that you won't have any children because it definitely causes birth defects. It's so serious that the National Institute of Mental Health is involved. It can have serious effects on the central nervous system. Much is still being determined about this drug. It works, but it will be a process. I know you really want this drug, but I will not allow you to make a decision today. Go home and read this packet. Come back next week and—"

I interrupted him. "Next week? No sir. I can sign now."

He ignored me and looked at his nurse. "Schedule her for next week, and we will go from there."

The walk to the car was slow. I thought, "Why is this man making me wait another week?" As soon as I got back to my apartment, I sat on my bed, glanced at the packet, and signed my name on the dotted line. I didn't care what I had to go through. I just wanted to be back to normal, and this was the quickest way.

It was a Friday afternoon, and I didn't have to work for several days. I stayed in my apartment all weekend, resting my face from makeup and drowning it in extra-strength acne creams, to no avail. Monday morning, I looked the same, probably with even more cysts and lesions. I couldn't wait for Friday. I'd determined this would be the last week of me looking like a monster. I canceled as many sessions as I could and wore a hat to the ones I couldn't cancel. I lied and said I had an outdoor event I was just leaving or going to. Teachers believed me and actually complimented me on my hat and comfortable clothing.

I was determined to hide until it was all over. I knew I was on the verge of losing my main job of going into the schools, but I just couldn't go, especially when nodules covered my face and hats weren't allowed. I stayed home. But for the first time, I stopped worrying about the future, because I knew this new miracle drug would change everything. And no one—and I do mean *no one*—could stop me from taking it, unless God Himself made it crystal clear not to take it.

CHAPTER 10

WHEN GOD SPEAKS

The night before my dermatologist appointment, I had a dream. I hadn't really asked God for His direction in whether to sign the agreement to take the new medication, just as I didn't ask Him when I first went to the dermatologist. I assumed I didn't have to, since I knew healing was His will for my life. That's what the Bible says, right? I stood on that, understanding that God can also use medicine to bring about healing.

For many other decisions, I was accustomed to hearing God's voice through a dream or through revelation. In fact, God spoke to me regularly through dreams. One time God spoke to me this way, it made me see Him in a really different way. It was one of the reasons I would *always* obey God when He gave me a dream or a vision.

This mind-blowing and memorable experienced happened in 2003. I'd just moved to Michigan to begin my graduate degree. I didn't know anyone there and certainly wasn't used to the weather. Winter was quickly approaching and being a Mississippi girl somewhat foreign to any real winter weather, I knew this experience was going to be different.

When I arrived at my dorm on campus, it was as if I'd stepped right into chaos. I was originally assigned a room in a graduate dormitory. However, when I got there, they told me the graduate dorms were full, and I'd have to stay in an undergraduate dorm, with an undergraduate roommate. And let me tell you, it was like a scene from a movie. There was screaming and hollering from every single floor of the building, and I was thinking, "No, I can't do this." After spending my first night in the room with my new roommate—a freshman, who seemed very uncomfortable with my race—I thought, "Oh no, I *really* can't do this!"

Throughout the night, I was awakened to her bear snores and funky farts filling the room; it smelled like an elephant's den at the zoo. I was miserable and couldn't see myself staying in that room or dormitory another night. The next day, I went to speak with a member of the residential staff, only to be met with a bad attitude. The lady told me I was lucky to even have a room, because others were on a waiting list. I walked away, and a tear fell down my cheek. I felt like I was living a nightmare.

I bugged that same lady several times after that, because my living situation was horrible, and I had a rigorous school schedule. Still no room vacancy. I was in an unfamiliar place, far from ideal, with no relief in sight. So I did the only thing I knew to do: I prayed. I asked God for help. I reminded Him that He'd promised in His Word to make my crooked places straight (Isaiah 45:2) and that I needed to be able to focus as I studied.

That night, in the midst of my roommate using the bathroom every hour and our next-door neighbors apparently studying to be a rock band, I had a dream. It was more like a vision, because I really don't remember how I was able to fall asleep with all the noise, horrible fart sounds, and smells. Whichever the case, I started dreaming, and in the dream an angel appeared to me. The angel told me to follow him, and I got up from my bed. He guided me up one flight of stairs in my dorm and then a second flight. When we got to the third floor, it looked empty. So I started walking down the hallway. I looked back, and the angel was still at the stairway. So I turned around and said, "Okay, sorry. Take me where you want me to go." The angel then walked me up to the fourth floor and to the very end of the hallway. He pointed to a room door. Then I woke up.

I remembered the dream and the room number the angel had pointed to. I felt as if he were telling me the room was empty. So I jumped up to get dressed and ran to the fourth floor to look at the room the angel had pointed out to me. "Was this really a dream? Is this someone's room, or am I just being crazy and desperate?" I thought. I knocked on the door, but no one answered. It was locked.

I walked away, battling with myself. Should I go to the administration office and talk with someone about that specific room or just ignore the dream? The lady had already told me several times that no more rooms were available. I thought, "Who am I kidding? I should just go to class." So I did. I walked halfway across campus to the graduate school buildings, which felt like walking five miles. When I finally arrived, there was a note on the door: "Class Cancelled." "This isn't happening right now! Now what?" I talked myself into walking to the administration office where the residential department was. It was right across the street from where I was standing, class was cancelled, and I had nothing else to do. I said to myself, "Why not try it?"

When the residential staff lady saw me again, she rolled her eyes, "How can I help you this time? As you know, we are booked for single rooms." I swallowed and cleared my throat, pulling out the sheet of paper I'd written the dorm room number on. I took a moment, looked at her with confidence, and said, "Ma'am, I know that this may sound crazy, but can you check this room that's located on the fourth floor of my dorm to see if it is available?"

"What? Sweetie, I told you that..."

"Listen, I know, but can you just check for me? Please."

At first the lady looked confused and slowly turned around to her computer. Her entire demeanor changed as she typed, ready to *prove* me wrong and get me out of her face. She snatched the sheet of paper from her desk where I'd placed it, inputted the information, and made her last click. She sat back, just waiting for her screen to show "OCCUPIED," but "VACANT" popped up on her screen instead. She sat up, clicked off the screen, and started the process again, assuming she'd entered the wrong number. I simply sat there and watched. Honestly, I, too, thought that maybe, just maybe, she'd keyed in the wrong number. This time she asked me to verify the number on the paper. I called out the number, and again "VACANT" appeared across her screen.

The smile on my face could have lit the entire room. I couldn't believe it. It was definitely a God thing for me. I sat in awe, and so did the lady. She turned and looked at me, questioning how I knew. I thought, "Should I tell her I had a dream? That an angel guided me up to the fourth floor of my dorm to that room, and that I actually went to that room when I woke up? Naahhhh." I just told her that someone from the room next to it told me they'd never heard anyone exiting or entering, so I decided to give it a try. She looked at me, left to grab the keys to my new room, and offered to drive me there to double-check. I stood there like a proud princess, knowing that my Heavenly Father had guided me. It felt good. It felt surreal.

We arrived at the room to find it totally empty—nothing but a bed and dresser. The lady apologized with a smile. She actually appeared happy for me, because she knew how miserable I was. Now I had a single room. Although I was still in an undergraduate dorm, the new room was quiet and just for me. I had no problems and later found out that many of the fourth-floor residents were also graduate students. As I moved my things, I thanked God for His guidance and direction. I vowed to never doubt His guidance for my life—whether through dreams or visions—ever again. This experience and many other similar ones were why I took the dream I had the night before my dermatologist appointment extremely seriously.

Nightmare or Vision?

Friday morning, the day of the much-anticipated dermatologist visit, I woke up from a disturbing dream. The closer time inched toward my appointment, the more I thought about it. I'd been asking God to speak to me for a while, as I was going through the battle with my skin. I had been waiting for a dream, a vision, anything that would give me direction on what to do. As I alluded to earlier, God had always guided me in the past, and the only way I wouldn't take this new miracle drug would be if God Himself stopped me. This dream seemed to be doing just that. I was distraught.

In the dream, I sat surrounded by children and teenagers. As I got up to walk, I saw that I was about nine months pregnant. I was absolutely beautiful and glowing. Out of nowhere, a pill was given to me. I took it, and everyone around me started to die—first the children and teens, then my own child within me. I cried out, "What's happening?" Then I heard the words, "The Enemy is after your posterity," and I woke up. I remember thinking, "What in the world does *posterity* mean?" I'd never heard that word before. I jumped out of bed to grab a dictionary, still analyzing the dream, because it scared me. I loved working with teens and wanted to have children of my own. I didn't want to be the cause of people dying. So, I searched the dictionary to see if the word even existed.

"Pos... pos... posterity. Found it!" It read, "All future generations of people... the descendants of a person." "What does this have to do with me?" I questioned. Then I replayed the words I'd heard right after I'd taken the pill in my dream and after everyone started to die: "The Enemy is after your posterity." I thought, "The Enemy is after my future generations of people... my descendants?" Just then, I knew the pill represented the new medication I'd committed to take, the miracle drug that would give me my beauty and my life back—and I was angry!

Was God really telling me not to go? Was He instructing me to cancel my appointment? In the middle of getting dressed, I fell to the floor and screamed as if I'd lost all hope. How could God be leading me *not* to take the very medicine that would heal me and save me from my pain? Did He not see that I was hurting? I mean, to have something appear on my face and grow, day after day, was the most humbling and broken experience of my life. I hated looking in the mirror. I hated seeing people, especially "perfect-skinned" people. I couldn't see anything else when I looked at someone, and I was extremely self-conscious about how they saw me.

I continued to question how God—a supposedly good God—could allow nodules and cysts to appear on my face. I, Chara, was known as the "goody-two-shoes girl." I, Chara, was the one waiting on marriage before intimacy. I followed all the rules. Now, I had no chance. Who would want me in such a state? I was furious. Getting up from the floor and still agonizing over the decision to obey or ignore God, I crawled back into my bed, questioning every single thing I ever believed about Him.

Posterity

I wasn't happy to hear from God that day, but I needed to figure out the *purpose* of posterity being mentioned in the dream. What was God referring to? What generation? *My* future generation from *my* bloodline or from others? Or maybe both? What did this mean for *me*? I didn't know it at all then, but I now know that every single thing I was getting ready to go through and *grow* through wasn't for me; it would be for future generations. Although what was to come would be a very hard and extremely grueling process, I would soon discover a truth that is needed now more than ever before. This truth would be the gift that would set me free from a negative self-image during the worst season of my life and would be my gift to future generations.

PART TWO

CHAPTER 11

MY BREAKING POINT

I really want to tell you I was happy and encouraged after realizing God was leading me down a different path of healing instead of taking the miracle drug, but I wasn't. I woke up sad and confused. I struggled with whether the dream was really from God or if it was just me. Truth is, I went back and forth with my decision. But I knew not to ignore the dream. Because of my experiences with dreams in the past, I knew to wait for God to give me clarity. The dream disturbed me and caused enough fear that I decided not to go through with the new drug. Deep down, I was grateful for direction, but mad and sad at the same time. I refused to even talk to God. How could I? I was so convinced that, of all people, I shouldn't be the one battling with a skin condition. After all, I had a close relationship with God—or so I thought.

The hardest part of my journey was facing the public, especially people who were drop-dead gorgeous, without a flaw in sight. To add to my misery, the workplace had become extremely difficult. Hiding was no longer an option for me. This was the job that I loved so much; my first real job—my main job. The one that allowed me to travel to high schools in rural areas to speak to teens. We had a new boss at the company, and not only was he demanding more staff meetings, but he was also calling the schools to make sure we were there during our scheduled hours, which were now set by the office. One day, my boss left a message on my voice mail that said, "Chara, this is a mandatory meeting, and if you are not here at this meeting, then you will have to suffer the repercussions of not showing up."

The company made big changes, and I had to comply. At the face-to-face meetings, I sat with my head down, often looking at the clock and fully aware of the cysts on my face. I was too uncomfortable to look up at others, especially when I knew they would glance at me every now and then and see my face. After the meetings, one of my coworkers would always whisper, "You still cute." It made me smile and feel better. I would hear this sentiment often from close friends and family. Although I appreciated the support, I couldn't imagine how I could be cute or beautiful in any way, given my extremely imperfect skin. Every day I woke up in a state of sadness and confusion as to why God was allowing me to go through something that was breaking me down daily.

Raina

One day at the headquarters for my main job, I felt an emotion I'd never felt before. It was the day Raina walked in. She had beautifully thick, black, bouncy hair that fell to her shoulders. Her smile was contagious, and she stood with confidence. She wore a cute dress (one I had in my closet as well) that accentuated her perfectly fit body. Her skin was flawless, and her teeth were perfect. She was introduced as someone truly special at her job, the new addition to the team. Immediately, I cringed. I wanted to leave, to cry, to run. I mean, this chick was beautiful! That emotion I felt had a name: jealousy.

I wasn't jealous just because she was pretty, but because she was pretty *and* she was my exact skin tone, size, and height. The boss told us she would be visiting us at our schools. I rolled my eyes and held my head down, not wanting her to come see my face up close. I'd seen other beautiful individuals in my life, but what made me so jealous of her was that she looked like the perfect version of me, living in the same city and town. She was who I wanted to be. She was who I felt I *should* be. She was the vision of my cry to God: "God heal me, and I will look like her—perfect." I had once lived in a season of beauty when I loved my look, height, size, and skin. I imagined that if I were still in that season, this new chick and I would have been the best of friends. We'd be two chicks hitting the town together, soaking up all the attention in our cute, neatly fitted attire. We'd walk into rooms together and turn heads. She was my vision of a perfect friend, and together we'd change the world in a fashionable and meaningful way. We would be two chocolate girls, running things. My twin sister didn't live in the same town, and at that time, I didn't have a friend that I hung out with daily.

There was a time where dark-skinned girls weren't seen as beautiful, but that was changing with ladies like Nia Long and Gabrielle Union stepping on the scene. Dark-skinned girls were being recognized as beautiful in the media. This was big for me, because I'd felt for so long that women with darker complexions were viewed as ugly—but now they were beautiful, even in music videos. Still, these women all had one thing in common: physical perfection. When you saw them, they had the perfect everything—skin, teeth, buttocks, and hair. Dark-skinned girls in the media were winning, but I still compared myself to them, thinking I could look just like them, if only God could touch my face and heal me.

That's how I saw Raina. She was fashionable like Gabrielle Union, had swag like Nia Long, and was physically perfect like Regina King. She had a presence when she walked in the room. My sadness turned into depression, and somewhere in-between lurked jealously.

My Most Embarrassing Moment

I heard Raina say, "Is Chara here? Is she available?" It was her first day visiting my school. I had just finished presenting to five classes at a middle school and was preparing for lunch before I finished my next three classes. I didn't want to walk in the cafeteria and sit with the students. I wasn't confident enough to be in a big room with hundreds of middle school students looking at me, but I had to do that as I taught. This new boss had my hands tied. Given that reality, during lunch I stayed behind in the classroom to just give myself a mental break.

She stood at the door, asking a teacher to direct her to me. The teacher turned and pointed, "There's Ms. Chara right there." Cringing, I looked up and rolled my eyes. I thought to myself, "Why is she looking for me? Why is she here?"

She approached me with the most beautiful smile in the world and introduced herself. I didn't want her to sit down by me. I didn't want her to get a close-up and analyze my face, because I didn't want to be reminded of how beautiful I could look if I had skin like hers. Every time I looked at her, she reminded me of what I lacked.

She was set to become a presenter as well, but for a different area, and they'd sent her to shadow the best—*me*. I was short with her and told her I was very busy, which I wasn't. I gave her other dates to shadow me, thinking maybe my skin would be better then. I didn't want to be watched, interviewed, or shadowed. It was hard enough facing teens daily; adding her to the equation made me feel even more uncomfortable. I didn't know how to be content with my condition. I didn't know how to appropriately persevere. So I lied to her and told her that another day would be better, and it worked. She agreed to see me another day.

I felt as if I was never ready for a full day with severe acne. I always wanted to just get home. Fighting through that day with lesions on my face was mentally and physically tiring, but I couldn't go home right after school that day. I had one more battle to face—a dinner meeting.

I sat at the dinner with working professionals, pretending to have fun. I talked and laughed, even though I didn't want to. "Chara, exert energy. Be present, push through," I thought. I made more conversation. I'm sure many stared at me, wondering about my skin. But I kept at it.

But then I noticed that when I talked no one looked at me. They started turning away. "This *wasn't* happening when I first sat at the table," I thought. I questioned what was causing others to turn from me? What I discovered in this moment would be etched in my mind for life. It would be the reason I later formed a habit of looking in the mirror every five minutes, sometimes every two minutes, to check my face. During the dinner meeting, I must've laughed too hard or moved my muscles too much while eating, because one of the cysts on my face decided it wanted to release itself right there as I made conversation. For a while I was unaware of it, but when I finally realized what was happening, I was extremely embarrassed and mortified. I wanted to crawl in a corner and die. In case you didn't already know, cysts are filled with pus-like fluids, and the dinner table is not exactly the place to see something such as my face releasing pus.

"God, why? Why are you doing this to me?" I questioned continuously on the way home. I cried in my car and on the way up the staircase of my apartment. I showered, washed my face with cleansing creams, and when my head finally hit the pillow, I just cried and cried some more, still asking, "Why me?"

The next morning was no different. I cried as I got up to get dressed. I sometimes had to stop completely to just sit and cry. I was scheduled to present to seven classes, and that meant facing more students. Needless to say, I wept more on the way to work. My strategy for the day was simple. I had several mirrors on me, big and small, and I vowed I would never again be embarrassed like I was the night before. My goal was to look at my face before others did. My obsession with mirrors had begun.

This wasn't to be vain but to prevent embarrassing moments from reoccurring. I remember a spiritual mentor noticed my obsession with looking in the mirror. He said to me, "God is going to deliver you from the mirror one day." I laughed and said, "That would be nice." That's how much I looked in mirrors.

I constantly pulled out a mirror at dinner, and every time I went out to eat, with or without someone, I'd put a small mirror on the table. I was obsessed, to say the least.

I kept trying to forget the horrible scene from the night before. I thought all night and the next day about what had happened at the dinner table. I mean, someone could have whispered, "Chara, look in the mirror." So many thoughts ran through my mind as I walked into the school, forcing myself to be ready to teach. Looking in the mirror during my teaching sessions became my norm as well. I didn't want to be embarrassed in front of the teens. I was mentally exhausted, paranoid that it would happen again. Mirrors were my safety net.

I just wanted to hurry up, get the day over with, and go back into my hiding place—my apartment. But mental exhaustion hit another level when I walked into the room to teach, because guess who was waiting on me? Beautiful Raina! "You ready?" she asked, smiling and excited, seemingly without a care in the world. I turned away from her to walk to the bathroom, with thoughts of my most embarrassing night, of my deepest desires, and of how sitting with her reminded me of my greatest need. I found an empty stall, closed the door, and cried, "God... see me and heal me... please!" It was in that moment that I felt like giving up.

I wanted to end my life. Life wasn't fun, it wasn't pleasurable, and it wasn't worth living for me anymore. "God, how can I leave this stall and face her? How can I like me with a face full of lesions? How am I supposed to get through this?" A "don't care" mentality started to form: "I don't care about life, about my job—I don't care about nothing and no one." I wiped my tears, marched back into the room, and rescheduled with Raina once again. I cancelled my classes, told the teacher I would need to leave earlier due to an emergency, and left the building.

CHAPTER 12

WHAT SHALL I DO?

My skin issues consumed me. I became so overtaken by them that turning on the TV, looking through magazines, and even meeting new people grew to be a deep challenge. Watching TV was the worst. No one on television appeared to have bad skin, and every time I watched, I envied someone's face. I would later find out that television production cameras have built-in filters. So, even if a person had bad skin, the cameras could easily filter their flaws. If only that were the case in real life.

Facebook became a global phenomenon around the time I was in the midst of my skin struggles. Guess who wasn't on Facebook? And you can probably guess why not. I was still struggling with cystic acne by age twenty-six. I hated taking pictures, and Facebook and other social media outlets were all about your perfect face and your appearance.

Everywhere I went, I saw another Raina, and I felt like my world wasn't fair. I remember being around my cousin at a family event. She had skin like a baby's bottom. She started to complain about a bump on her face. The bump she described to me was barely noticeable—nonexistent, even. Yet, she went on and on about it. I wanted to cry, to switch places with her. Didn't she see me? Why in the heavens would *she* be complaining—and to *me*, of all people?

I was reaching my breaking point. I didn't want to think. I didn't want to live. I didn't want to move forward; my imperfections had caused me to retreat. They caused me to want to be removed from people, from places, and from doing the things I loved. I was no longer confident and found myself slipping deeper and deeper into depressive moods. I knew I was slipping when I saw a huge, ugly bug crawl toward me as I sat outside one day, and I just stared. I know that sounds crazy, but normally I would have run, screamed, stepped on the bug, or quickly moved out of the way. I hated bugs of any kind. But on that day, I didn't care. I just sat there, emotionless, as it crept up my leg. On another occasion, I missed the biggest mandatory meeting for the office because of my skin. I lied and said I was out of town for a family emergency. The boss called me and asked if I could call in to the meeting. The US government's administration was changing, and the grant that funded my job was being affected. But I didn't care. I lay in bed listening to the voice mail and never called back.

By this time in my skin struggle, putting on makeup was a *must*! Every acne bump left a dark mark, so my face was *three* shades darker than normal because of the scarring, and I no longer recognized myself in the mirror without makeup. Once, someone really close to me accidentally saw me without makeup when she came by to visit unannounced. I ran in the bathroom and fixed up my face. When I emerged, she told me I really needed to send a before-and-after picture to the makers of the brand of makeup I was using, because no one would believe how well it covered my discoloration. Emotionless, I stared at her. I felt like a stranger to myself: "Who is this girl, and what's happening to her world?"

I was so far from pretty—or shall I say, perfection—that I just wanted to give up trying, give up living, give up on it all. It was impossible for me to be *me*. I thought I could totally be myself once I *looked* like myself again. I believed that society's definition of beauty was something I had to obtain in order to be successful and accepted. It was all I wanted. But by this point in my life, I'd settle for simply looking average, with normal skin.

I cried uncontrollably every morning and every night. I couldn't see past my flaws. I didn't have normal days. Twenty-four hours of the day, I longed to return to my normal appearance. But since I couldn't, I was headed for destruction. Truth is, I needed a revelation. I needed to know that beauty went way beyond the word "pretty." I needed to know I was still valuable and that there was something more worth living for, despite how I looked. I contemplated, "If beauty is all about the outward appearance, then maybe I should just kill myself now." In that moment, depressed and seriously contemplating ending it all, I became a statistic.

Suicidal

I lay in bed, staring at the ceiling as tears flowed from my eyes and soaked my pillow. "God, I know You are there. You promised to never leave me. Why do I look like a monster? Why am I going through this? I just want to know why. That's all. Please tell me. *Why?*"

By this time, I'd been struggling with my skin condition for over four years since the pills first stopped working for me. I needed to hear from God and understand what was happening to me. I felt as if I were going crazy. Negative thoughts started to consume me, and my actions followed. I knew I was going down a seriously dangerous path. I was very aware of my emotions and knew I needed to get a grip on them because the negative voices I was hearing were loud and very real. I started having suicidal thoughts throughout the day and night. And because it wasn't the first time I'd experienced hearing negative voices or contemplated suicide, I knew I needed help.

The first time I lost control of my mind was back in college, and no one ever knew. I should have run for help, but I was too scared. I never told a single soul I'd had a mental breakdown stemming from hearing negative voices. The trouble started with a simple thought, but turned into something very serious, very quickly. The thoughts I was currently having reminded me of what had happened in the past, and it scared me.

The First Time

It was my senior year in college when I first had thoughts of suicide—in the midst of play production and the grueling coursework required to graduate. I had big plans for the year, especially for the production, when suddenly I woke up one day with a deep feeling of sadness, along with intense, negative thoughts on my mind. The thoughts were loud, like audible voices. The sad part is that I actually believed what I heard: "You're worthless, Chara. You have no friends; no one likes you. You can't do this."

The thoughts started off as small suggestions that left me feeling *less than*. They continued until one morning I woke up with the thoughts intensified. The next day I had a thought that I was physically sick and dying. It's hard to explain, but I thought, "Oh God, I'm dying." These thoughts or voices then suggested I'd be better off killing myself, rather than dying slowly. It got to the point where it was like a psychotic episode. Delusions became real to me; hallucinations were occurring. I could feel the struggle. I lost control of my reality and my mental state. This went on for a full week, causing severe mental pain, to where I couldn't function normally. Talk about being confused and wanting to be free.

Dying was my only option to be free—or so the voices suggested. I couldn't focus in class. I even pushed back the production date. I actually thought I had a severe physical illness, yet without any physical symptoms. I knew *something* was wrong, but I was afraid to share anything, because I felt sharing it would make things worse. I thought I would seem crazy (and, in reality, I *was* suffering mentally). I was in extreme emotional pain from the thoughts that kept playing in my head. I went from having a desire to die, but without a specific plan, to developing an actual plan to kill myself.

I went home to visit my mom. I couldn't bear the thought of seeing my dad because I thought it would be harder for me to go through with my plan if I saw him. While at home, I told my mom that I loved her and went in my old childhood room to write a goodbye letter to her. I placed it under my bed, so she'd be able to find it after I went through with my plans. Even while in my room, I was fighting to get back in my right mind, to tell myself that life wasn't that bad, that I wasn't sick, that all was well. But I kept hearing negative thoughts, and the voices seemed to scream louder.

I left my mom's house to go back to my dorm room. My sister was my roommate at the time, but she never stayed there at night. She was often at her guy friend's house or with her best friend on campus. I planned to take action the next day. I cried myself to sleep. The next morning, I had my favorite class, but it was time for me to act on my plan. I was serious. I'd plotted my plan to a *T* and decided to write a small letter to God right before it was time to carry it out:

> God, I really don't know what's going on. I can't shake this. I grew up in church hearing that you are a good God and a real God. But I don't see any awesomeness. Sorry for this.

I folded the paper and walked toward the door, ready to end my life. As I opened the door, I felt determined to go through with it, strong-willed and strong-minded. I felt it was the only option, and no one could help me. Surely, telling anyone would make it worse. "I'm doing the right thing and all the mental pain will be over soon." These thoughts were real to me; they were confusing and clouding my judgment. I knew something was wrong but felt I couldn't escape the thoughts. As I opened the door, tears flowing from my eyes, I promise you I heard an audible voice say, "I am the Lord God, strong and mighty, and I will show you just who I am." And suddenly, all the negative voices scattered.

Immediately, I felt peace—immediately! I stood still and realized I was free from the voices. It was as if something physically lifted from my shoulders and from my mind. I fell to my knees and wept. My mental pain was gone; it was like I was back to reality in an instant. I could think clearly and refute every negative thought I'd heard. I had taken my mental health for granted all my life. But those two weeks changed my life; they changed me mentally. And for the first time, I wanted to discover more about "the voice" that spoke to me. This voice healed me. It regulated my mind. I knew the voice was God, and I needed to know more about this God. I needed to know about the God who could, in an instant, snap me back into my right mind. This God became real to me.

Around this same time, when my twin sister and I shared college dorm rooms, she would walk in the room at four in the morning, sometimes ready to go to sleep after all-night partying, sleepovers with her bestie, or doing whatever else she wouldn't want me to say. And every time she walked in the room from that day forward, she found me sitting in my chair reading my Bible. She never knew what drove me to that chair at 4 a.m.; she simply respected it. Well... to be more exact, she walked in, rolled her eyes, jumped into bed, and went to sleep. Reading my Bible became my morning routine. Growing up in church, I learned that the best way to get to know God is to read His will found in the Bible, but I never did so until then. I just wanted to know more and more about the voice that healed my mind, and reading the Bible brought me closer to understanding God.

I was super excited that God had spoken to me. I wanted to know more about Him, and every morning since that day I've woken up and dived into my Bible. I was intrigued. I didn't know it at the time, but I was establishing my personal relationship with God and building a foundation that would prevent me from succumbing to future negative thoughts and suggestions.

As I read, I started with stories in the Old Testament. I would read about David and Goliath, Daniel in the lions' den, and other stories I'd heard in Sunday school but never read for myself. It felt like I was watching a dramatic TV show, especially when I read the stories of Sodom and Gomorrah and the like. I'm telling you, it was like, "Let's see the drama and juiciness occurring today... Where is my Bible?"

My favorite story in the Bible is the story of Moses in the book of Exodus. I studied his life and his relationship with God. I was so intrigued with how God's power worked for Moses and the children of Israel, with how ten tormenting plagues were placed on the Egyptians who enslaved them. The tenth plague was deadly. Reading to myself I thought, "God is one bad mamma jamma!" Each time I read about a plague, I thought, "Now that's some type of power. Wow! That same power, that same God, is the God that spoke to me. That's the same God that now lives within me. That's the God I serve? He really is powerful." That's how I read Bible stories. I didn't read them just to read. I wanted to truly understand the power of this great God I served.

Second Time Around

When I started having suicidal thoughts again because of the issues with my skin and a negative self-image, I knew not to allow those thoughts to linger. I knew it was time to put an end to them. I'd already started contemplating a suicide plan. So I sat up on my bed and started speaking to God aloud, to the God who had healed my mind before, to the God I'd spent time with, learning about how powerful He was and is. I started begging Him to speak to me, to heal me. I felt the emotional pain returning. I needed Him to bring healing to my skin. I needed that God to start explaining to me why I, of all people, was going through this. I waited. All that week, I sat on my bed, cried, and waited. I screamed, I wailed, I cried aloud, as if I were in physical pain—which I sometimes was, due to my skin condition. I needed that

God from my senior year to speak to me once more.

For a full week, I got no response. No voice from God, no audible experience, nothing. Just the sound of me sniffling. Then something happened. I grew tired of crying, though tears still flowed as I sat up and gathered my strength. I thought about the God who was once real to me. I put myself in remembrance of all the experiences I'd had with Him and uttered these words:

God, I'm not crazy. I know that You're real because You've healed my mind before. I know that You're real because I have the memories of all of those Bible stories I once read for myself. You were for those people in Bible times. You never left any of them, and I will believe that You will never leave me. Maybe, just maybe… maybe You're trying to teach me something. Maybe You have a purpose behind it all. Because in every story that I've ever read in the Bible, there was a purpose for people's pain, there was a purpose for each trial, and You always showed up. Maybe, just maybe, if I get the message, then my healing will manifest. Maybe, just maybe, You're up to something? I believe that. I must be like one of your disciples, and there must be a plan in the end. So God, even though this hurts, I need to tell You this:

God, I trust You.

I trust that You know what You are doing. I trust that You see me and that You care. Even though this hurts, I trust You. Please just show me Your will.

With those words, I turned over and cried myself to sleep, not knowing I had just changed the trajectory of my life.

CHAPTER 13

LET THE HEALING BEGIN

The next morning, my mind-set was different. I washed my face differently, speaking aloud to myself a lot. I would say, "Chara, all is well," even though it wasn't. While putting on my makeup, I said, "My face is healed, and I'm camera ready." I didn't want to be sad, and I was tired of crying, tired of asking God to heal me every single day. It actually made the acne worse. I was simply determined—determined to discover my why. Why am I going through this? Was God trying to show me something? What was on the other side of this? What was God trying to teach me, tell me, or show me? I knew the quicker I could get the message, the quicker my trial could possibly be over. I was on a new mission, and I refused to wake up unhappy on a daily basis. It was time for a new way of doing things, a new mentality. I didn't really know how to start, but I woke up determined not to be sad.

I researched healthy eating habits and loving oneself from within. The healthy eating tips helped me, as I changed everything about my diet. I threw away junk foods, sugar, white bread, and anything that caused inflammation. I purchased healthy foods and started exercising. I became a little extreme in that season of my life, but I saw a difference. My acne was hormonal more than anything, but the healthy eating actually helped with the inflammation. I wasn't walking around with huge lesions on my face every single day. The boils and cyst came but were not as inflamed as before. However, my scarring became extremely evident. So I searched for treatment creams weekly.

No book was able to reach me and help me with what I was going through. They couldn't help me love myself more, so I threw them away. Any book that suggested I look in the mirror and declare that I was beautiful got thrown away, because when I looked in the mirror, I saw lesions. I needed something deeper, something that went beyond my physical assets. I was determined to walk in my healing, though I didn't yet understand that *inner* healing had to come first. How my inner healing began wasn't quite what I expected, but I was finally in a place to receive it.

Two to three weeks after changing my diet, I had a serious breakout. It was one that would normally cause me to stay in my apartment. About four inflamed lesions appeared on my face. My new mind-set was immediately tested when I received a call to teach several hundred students at one of my old schools. I'd hoped the lesions would go down before the date I was set to speak. Well, the date arrived, and the lesions were still there. I cried. Honestly, I screamed and kicked myself all the way to the school. I asked the same question as before, "God, why?" not knowing that I would receive a hint of the answer by day's end.

Even though I washed my face differently and put on my makeup with proclamations of healing, I still hated living with cysts on my face. Just because I was determined and had a new mind-set toward what I was facing, it didn't mean I wanted it to continue. I couldn't believe the breakout I had. As soon as I got to the school, I rushed straight to the restroom to see if my face was really that inflamed. "Maybe a different mirror will show me differently," I thought. I truly believed that. That day, I had about four different mirrors of all sizes on me.

When I walked into the school, even the teacher questioned, "Chara, are you okay?" She saw how I looked. No one had ever seen me at my worst like that—*ever*! She frowned and seemed really concerned. That's how crazy I looked. To this day I can't even explain how or why I kept walking into the school, but I did. The new boss I had didn't make it easy for me to cancel. The teachers were reporting to headquarters whether I showed up or not. Usually, that would have been a day I'd have definitely canceled. It could've been that I knew I couldn't afford to miss any more days, or I'd be fired. Or it could've been my inner determination.

Either way, walking into the school that day was a real struggle. I went back and forth mentally. I walked into the large classroom to start my presentation. I had six classes in all and had to face a full group of new students over and over again. The more I thought about it, the more frightened I became.

When the first group of students walked into the room, I turned to pack my bags. I felt as if I couldn't do it. My stomach started to turn, and I was turning with it—turning all the way to the car. I grabbed my keys and started packing. I picked up my bag to walk out of the door. But just then, something happened. I heard the voice I had been longing to hear from, the voice I was seeking answers from, the voice I had cried out to throughout those lonely nights. It was God's voice again. He challenged me: "Chara, what if this is the one message that could change the course of each person's life sitting before you? What if this is the one message that could transform the nation by them simply hearing you?"

I was truly touched. I dropped my keys and at that moment remembered that I was graced to give my gifts, despite my imperfections and insecurities. I remembered the day I wrote down my gifts and talents on a sheet of paper, professing I needed a change, that I needed to be in front of teens, using my gifts. I was created to create and present to teens. It's what I did very well. I remembered that God saw me, and He had a purpose for me, even in my pain. And just maybe, He was up to something.

I turned around to go ahead and face my students. I confidently announced, "Forgive me for my breakout, but I will still have class." Some laughed and said, "It's okay, Ms. Chara." I could feel the frowns of others. I'm pretty sure the teacher would have allowed me to go home if I'd told her I wasn't feeling well, because I *looked* like I wasn't feeling well. This wasn't a regular acne breakout. The lesions were really inflamed that day. Staying was the challenge. I persevered and gave my first audience all of me, as if nothing were wrong. What happened next started my transformation.

The students enjoyed my presentation. They enjoyed it so much that some didn't want to leave. Some approached me for more insight and gave me accolades, handshakes, and hugs. Most of all, they affirmed that my message was life changing. Although I taught the facts about sexually transmitted diseases (STDs) and shared shocking STD statistics, I also shared real-life stories of people from their age group affected with incurable sexually transmitted diseases. The stories I told were revealing and personal. I had once interviewed teens infected with STDs and received their permission to share their stories. I told each story as if it were the interviewee's final message to any teen who would listen. All the stories challenged teens to consider their worth and value when making decisions. They were shocked to hear about a thirteen-year-old student infected with HIV and herpes after her first sexual encounter. You could hear a pin drop toward the end of every class. The room was just that quiet, as if each teen were rethinking his or her past careless decisions.

When class was over, no one treated me like I had a disease or as if I were contagious. (Well, the ones that did left the building right after the presentation). Many saw beyond my physical appearance. Yes, at the beginning they had judged me, and I felt it. But afterward there was a total difference. It was such a good feeling. And this feeling happened over and over after each class. I actually forgot about how I looked, and when I did remember, I was shocked. I ran to the restroom to look in the mirror (even though I had several on me). Were they talking and interacting with me with a face full of lesions? Did the lesions go down? What was going on? Nope, the lesions were still there.

That day, I walked into the school still secretly wanting my life to end, yet I left the school ready to live again. I had never experienced this type of happiness. It was indescribable. I spent the entire drive home reflecting. What had changed? I remembered making myself forget about how I *looked* to focus on what I was there to *do*. I wanted the teens to truly hear what I was saying, so that my presentation was effective. Yes, I taught on STDs that day, and to be honest, I looked like I could possibly have had all of them. I looked horrible. But the students' response transformed me. Truthfully, it *didn't* make me any more comfortable going out in public with lesions. Trust and believe, I still went straight home after school. But I went straight home with a different mind-set. I questioned, "Is this what real beauty looks like?" Then it hit me: "Is this what God is trying to teach me? Is this the mission? Is beauty beyond how I look?" I knew nothing different about external beauty than I'd believed all these years, but maybe I was about to find out a new perspective.

CHAPTER 14

IS THIS MISSION POSSIBLE?

Sometimes, in order to believe something, you must see it. In this case, it was as if God sent Tee right into my life as an example. Honestly, I'd never seen or met anyone who struggled with the type of acne I was experiencing—or even abnormal acne in general. I questioned if it was even possible to feel pretty with a messed-up face. More than that, I questioned if it was truly possible to feel and be secure and confident with physical imperfections. That all changed when I met Tee. I don't know if she realizes just how much her life, confidence, and boldness gave me hope. You never know who's watching you, and I was watching her.

    I saw Tee the day my mother had a small role in a theatrical production, and she asked me to come and support her. I didn't want to. I was focused on going to work despite my insecurities, but I tried not to go other places. But Mom said it would really make her happy if I came to support her, so I did. I got to the production and noticed that the main character was a beautiful, dark-skinned woman I went to college with. She always walked alone in college, and I remember wanting to get to know her. She did an outstanding job and really showed her flirty, seductive side in her role as every guy's love interest in the production. After the play, I wanted to see her, but my mother wanted me to rush to a restaurant to celebrate her "big break" into show business. My mom didn't have a huge role, but just like in real life, she always stole the show.

While at the restaurant, to my surprise, I saw the young lady from the play. I called her name, trying to get her attention. She was walking in the opposite direction and didn't hear me, so I started approaching her. After pushing past a crowd of people, I was finally able to get close enough to tap her on the shoulder.

When she turned to look at me, I was caught off guard by what I saw. Her face was covered with acne—and I do mean covered. With a smile, she greeted me and gave me a hug. Still, I was speechless. To keep from being rude, I quickly gathered my words and congratulated her on her starring role and told her what a wonderful job she had done. I was trying not to be impolite, because I understood all too well the shock many felt when they came close to me. She thanked me, turned back around, and left.

On the way home that night, I couldn't stop thinking about what I had witnessed. From a distance onstage, she looked perfect. She was onstage as the love interest of many and played her role perfectly. I never would have imagined that she had a face covered in acne. She didn't seem to care, though. This was absolutely shocking to me. Here I was, afraid to go anywhere, and this beautiful young lady, the same age as me, with the same skin tone, was the star of the night—with a face that looked similar to mine. Her acne was quite different—not as inflamed—but it was still acne.

How in the heck did she do that? How was she living without caring about the reactions of others? She was living her life without allowing her appearance to stop her. Playing this major role was proof of that. She was a true example to me. I had *never* witnessed anyone so pretty, with my skin tone, and so confident with imperfections. In a weird sense, I was happy to see that she wasn't perfect. She didn't look flawless like Raina, yet she was still a beautiful, dark-skinned woman. I'm pretty sure she noticed my skin that night, too. She may have forgotten about how I looked, but I could never forget her look. That night we spoke, hugged, and left each other's presence, but she would become my inspiration. She made me think, "Maybe this mission is possible. Can I really be confident and actually like me while waiting on my healing?"

My face was ever changing. I had slightly more good days, even with the continuing acne, because I changed my diet, causing breakouts not to be as inflamed. I wanted to get rid of the acne, period. Every day, my refrigerator looked like a forest. I ate lettuce for breakfast, lunch, and dinner. I went from pouring salads into a bowl to just walking around eating salad straight from the bag. I was determined to have clear skin, and if eating and exercising could help, I was on it daily. (At that time, I was a little extreme and lost a lot of weight just eating salads, but later learned how to balance out a healthy skin diet.) I was too afraid to join a gym, because I didn't want the delayed reaction of a guy approaching me from behind and then rejecting me when he got up close. So, I worked out at home. I drank plenty of water, using gallon jugs to determine whether I was drinking enough. I still had breakouts.

Later that year, I ran into Tee again—but this time at the office of a new dermatologist I'd found on the opposite end of town. To my surprise, her skin was flawless. "But how?" I asked. I didn't even bother to say "Hello" or "Hey girl, good to see you! How are you doing?" None of that. You see, when a person has really bad acne and meets another person with the same struggle, there's an automatic bond.

Tee immediately started sharing her secrets with me on how she'd perfected her skin. I lit up in excitement. We exchanged numbers and texted often about skin regimes. She gave me hope, not just that my skin could one day be free from acne but that I could love myself in the process.

We ran into each other again at a production held at one of Mississippi's performance art theaters. I was summoned to attend for one of my many jobs. While at the show, I stepped out of the production to go to a downstairs bathroom. As I walked the building, I noticed the elegance of the place, appreciating that there was no crowd to push through like there was before the show began. Admiring the elaborate double doors of the bathroom, I walked in and to my surprise, I saw Tee standing in front of the sink washing her hands. I was so happy to see her, and she seemed just as happy to see me. The bathroom was quite long, with immaculate countertops. Beautiful, massive mirrors surrounded the walls. We stood in front of the mirrors and talked. Our conversation deepened on that day. Before, we would see each other and just discuss skin regimes. But that night, Tee opened up to me about her off-and-on struggle with acne—how it affected her dating life and even her career aspirations in music. I assumed that because she was in several productions she didn't really care about her troubled skin. However, she did—yet refused to allow it to stop her. Even though she discussed her skin struggle, her face looked amazing on that day, and it encouraged me to keep striving toward my healing. I left that night calling her my angel, because it was as if God placed her in my path every time I needed a boost of encouragement. We hugged and left. It would be years later before we actually saw each other again face-to-face. But when we did, I discovered that Tee had pursued her career in music, and I was grateful to be invited to her CD release party. Once again, she was onstage in the forefront, and I admired that about her.

Tee and I never became close, close friends, nor did we hang out—although I really wanted us to. That just wasn't her personality, or maybe it wasn't the right time. However, a couple of years later from her CD release party (after I discovered the truth about beauty), I created a forum where women gathered for a panel discussion on fighting insecurities. She was my special guest, and I shared with her during the event just how much her lifestyle had impacted my life. Talk about tears! (Believe it or not, even Raina was invited and joined the discussion. We cried too.) What was so interesting about that gathering was that Tee and I both shared our insecurities from living with acne and how we discovered the truth about beauty, despite having severe imperfections. Of course, she reached her epiphany before me, but little did I know I would soon have the same revelation that caused her to get onstage and not be consumed by her insecurities. I didn't think it was even possible before meeting her.

My journey to discovering true beauty while living with my insecurities was just starting when I first ran into her at the dermatologist's office. She was coming to the end of her skin battle. My insecurities kept me from living, but seeing her live despite her insecurities and imperfections was all the motivation I needed. Today, I still enjoy hearing from Tee, and I honestly don't think she realizes how much she helped me through such a hard season of my life. Hopefully, she will when she reads this book. My hope is that this book will be that same inspiration and push for others to keep going, just as she provided for me.

The battle of wanting to be physically perfect was constant. And even though I was determined to trust and wait on God, it was still hard. "How can I get through this season with imperfections? How can I face the public?" These questions plagued my mind, but I thought about how Tee did it onstage. I became motivated even more to live and face people, regardless of how I looked. I didn't want to care about what others thought about my face and how I looked, especially on the days I looked like a monster. But that wasn't easy, and I was still confused as to *how* I could live like that with confidence. Even though I wasn't quite sure how to get there, I had a hope inside that it was truly possible.

One day Patricks called me. By this season of my life, we no longer worked at the alternative school together, and he'd moved to Providence, Rhode Island, to attend Brown University. However, we would talk all the time. He was like my little brother, but often when he would give me advice, it was like he'd transformed into my big brother. Patricks had a way with words. I called him Mr. CNN because he always sounded like a commentator who should be broadcast around the globe. He could explain things and challenge me in a way that made me look at him with awe. This phone call would be one of those conversations.

I expressed to Patricks my desire to get to a better emotional place on my bad breakout days, but the struggle was real. I told him that, deep down, I wanted to live past the feelings that would normally cause me to crumble, stay hidden, and wait until my skin was perfect. I shared with him my experience of watching Tee onstage and how I wanted that confidence. He listened and waited patiently as I finished expressing my thoughts. Then he simply asked me one question: "Chara, who are you?"

"What? I'm confused. What do you mean?"

"Chara, who are you when your face breaks out? Who are you when your hair falls out? Who are you if you gain weight, lose it all, find yourself alone, down-and-out? Who are you?"

"Wait... you want an answer?" I asked.

The most interesting thing happened. I couldn't answer him. I had no idea how to define *me*. I didn't know who I was, especially when I had a breakout, because my world would usually collapse. But maybe if I knew the answer to Patricks's question, I could take more control over the emotions that seemingly ran my world.

Patricks's question "Who are you when your face breaks out?" would play over and over in my head that night, long after our conversation was over. It was time to answer that question. I was really on a mission to discover how to live, how to break free from my insecurities and my body image dissatisfaction. I was tired of allowing the psychological effects of having acne to move me. So I strategically planned a day in which I would sit down and answer the question "Chara, who are you?"

CHAPTER 15

PROJECT ME

I decided I would spend time the next morning to sit down and think. "Who am I?" That morning, I sat in silence for a while. I really wanted to know the answer to that question, but no response stood out in my mind. I realized I had no clue *who* I really was. So, I took a different approach. I asked myself, "How would I discover someone else or get to know another person? How did I get to know Patricks?" I got to know him, and any other person in my life, by asking them questions. Then it hit me: "I will interview me."

I thought of questions and wrote them on paper. I even googled more creative questions and added them to my list. I decided to write all my questions down first before answering them. When I finished, it was night. I realized I had written ninety-six questions, and I was super excited to answer them all. I was so excited to take the full week to get to know me. I thought to myself, "If I have never, ever sought after what I like, dislike, love, or hate, then whose life have I been living?"

Chara, what is your favorite food?

Why do you HATE scary movies?

If you could do something different and exciting, what would it be, and why?

Chara, what do you want out of life?

> *Tell me three things you wish you had, and why.*
>
> *Girl, who is your crush?*
>
> *Describe the perfect guy to marry, just for you.*

I was so happy to answer each question. I found it fun and exciting to rush home to discover more and more about *me*. I was determined to discover Chara. I wrote down my responses, and I'm not talking about just one-sentence responses. I gave paragraph-long responses to each question. I wrote why I choose each answer. I laughed, cried, and even spoke aloud as I wrote down my answers.

> *If you could have dinner with a person, dead or alive, who would it be, and why?*
>
> *Five things you love to do...*
>
> *Something you want to try to do before leaving this world...*
>
> *Who do you admire, and why?*

I even asked myself specific questions based on my struggle:

> *Why do you dislike Raina?*
>
> *If you had clear skin, what would you be doing right now, at this very moment? Can you still do that now? What will happen if you do?*
>
> *How would your life change if you stopped hiding in this apartment?*

At the time, I didn't understand how answering such questions would impact me. I didn't want to just write a response to the questions. I wanted to respond with my life.

"If you had clear skin, what would you be doing right now, at this very moment?" I thought about this question a lot and really took my time in writing down what I would have been doing. My answer caused me to think and react. I had to be bold and make a move—to literally take action. And boy, did my life take a drastic turn when I did.

Project Do

It was a Saturday morning, and I wanted to be out experiencing new things with a diverse group of people. That was my answer to the question "What would you be doing if you didn't have a breakout or didn't care?" I wrote,

> *I would be out meeting people, a diverse group of people who are like-minded. I want to meet and get to know people who could walk with me and support me in life. Who could care less about how they look, or how I look. I want to meet good, solid, caring people who are just different.*

I wanted friends. I wanted to support others, to be there for them. I had been alone in my apartment, sitting in my room for too long—for years. And on that very day, I looked online to discover where I could go in Mississippi to meet a diverse group of people who would be nonjudgmental and have fun. It was important for me to be around the right people because I understood there were superficial people out there who would judge me for my imperfections. There were people who would have been so focused on their physical appearance that it would've made me feel like I couldn't measure up to their standards of beauty. Before, that's how I had lived daily, and I had grown tired of that mind-set. I didn't even realize I was moving away from society's standards of beauty and perfection. I just yearned to live without judgment while walking my path of healing.

I searched the internet to see where I could go to be around people who were like me or better. I saw that a ballet company was having a production that night at the downtown auditorium. *The Book of Ruth: A Dance Production* consisted of ballet and modern dancers acting out scenes from the Bible story. I thought it would be interesting. I went ahead and bought a ticket online to see the performance, acting quickly so I wouldn't change my mind. I was nervous and scared because I was pushing myself out of my comfort zone and challenging myself to be me. I had plenty of new outfits in my closet that I'd never worn, because I now hated dressing up. I had no excuses and no way out of the decision I'd made. The ticket was purchased, and I was scheduled to go by myself. That night, I dressed up in a comfortable, casual romper and put on four-inch heels. I felt cute. Even though I had a small breakout, I styled my hair, did my makeup, and said to myself, "Let's do this." I grabbed my keys and took one final look in the mirror. I couldn't believe I was actually preparing to go out to an event. Not just any event, but one outside of my comfort zone.

When I arrived, it was super crowded, an auditorium filled with more Caucasian Americans than African Americans. Mississippi wasn't—and still isn't—as diverse as other states, such as New York or California. I had lived and breathed my community and wanted to branch out and meet new people from different backgrounds. The mission was to go in, enjoy the show, and possibly meet a new friend. Ready for my new adventure, I boldly walked into the auditorium.

My seat was toward the front, in the middle of a group of people already seated. They were all on time, and I was a little late. The show was about to start, and there was my one measly seat, surrounded by a sea of Caucasians. Mississippi is known for its history of cruelty toward blacks, and to be honest, I was nervous. Even though we were far past that history, I had never built relations with others outside of my race, just as many others from that area hadn't. I thought to myself, "Will the white people want me to sit by them? Will they get up and move? Oh God... Was this the right idea? How is this getting to know me?" I was literally about to turn around and go home. At that moment, a young Puerto Rican lady (the only Puerto Rican in the auditorium) tapped me on my shoulder. I guess I had been standing in one spot, thinking, for too long. She spoke with a deep accent and stood with a camera in her hand. I had noticed her earlier, taking pictures of the stage and crowd.

"Hey, let me help you. What seat are you sitting in?"

I showed her my ticket.

"Oh, you're by my friends. You're by good people! Let me walk you to your seat and introduce you to them."

She pointed to my seat, and before I could say thank you and squeeze my way into my seat, she stopped me and got the attention of the whole crowd in that area, "Hey everybody! This is my new friend. Wait, what's your name?"

"I'm Chara."

"Hey everybody, my new friend Chara. Hey Chara, these are my friends, and you're sitting by the first lady of the church we all go to. Okay, everybody, make her feel welcome, because the show is about to start."

She patted me on the back, and I looked at her with a smile. I scooted my way to my empty seat. The fear of sitting by mean and cruel people left me. They all had smiles on their faces and bombarded me with beautiful greetings and questions like "Is this your first time seeing this performance?" They told me they had all seen the show twice. They seemed super sweet and shared that many of their friends were in the production. I smiled, nodded, and listened. I sat next to a pastor's wife, who was very sweet. As the show began and the lights dimmed, she whispered to me, "You will really enjoy this production. Trust me: it's touching."

She was right. The production was amazing. I laughed and cried all through it, interacting with the crowd that surrounded me. My seatmates checked on me from time to time to see if I was enjoying the show. And as I sat there, I felt something foreign to me: I felt happy. I felt like I was *living*—experiencing new things, talking to people, embracing their fondness of me. It was fun!

Here I was, crying through a dance production. The production was nothing but dance and movement, no talking. Every movement had an emotion matched with the perfect music. It reignited my passion for the arts. My senior year in college I'd produced two play productions. But when I developed the skin condition, I pushed my passion and love for the arts aside. It felt so good to be in that moment of remembrance and happiness.

During the intermission, the first lady invited me to her church. She told me that they'd just started a young adult Sunday morning class. I was excited and told her I would come. I couldn't believe I said YES! The thought to get to know them more interested me. When the show ended, the production received a thundering standing ovation. My entire section, including I, jumped up and beamed with joy with applause. I gathered my things and started to leave, and many in the section yelled, "See you tomorrow, Chara!" The first lady had announced that I was coming to their church and their new young adult class. How could I not?

The evening seemed perfect. And as I reflected on who I was sitting around, I took note that I wasn't around people who were judgmental or superficial. They didn't look me up and down when I walked in. They weren't focused on anyone's outward appearance. They were different. I'd just met them, but I was comfortable around them. Because of who they were, for the first time I forgot that I was battling with skin imperfections. I didn't feel judged. I felt comfortable, and I wanted more of that feeling.

CHAPTER 16

FRIENDS AND FREEDOM

It was Sunday morning, the very next day, and I was running late to the young adult class I'd been invited to while at the dance production. I looked in my closet to figure out what in the heck to wear. I didn't want to dress all the way up, just in a way that I could feel comfortable and cute. I'd become accustomed to hiding, so I was very careful not to stand out with my wardrobe. I wanted to deflect as much attention from myself as possible. My skin still had its good days and bad days, and this day was considered a good day —only a small breakout. I rushed out of my apartment, trying my best to make it on time to the class. I ended up late, but I was still excited—thrilled, even—to make new connections with such a diverse group of people. My project to get to know myself started opening doors that I had no idea existed. I couldn't believe that in a matter of a days, I went from hiding in my apartment to visiting a new church. I must say, I was proud of *me*.

When I arrived, I was guided to the room by a sweet stranger, and I slowly opened the door. Class was already in session. It was a group discussion, with each person expressing their opinions. As I sat down, I saw familiar faces from the night before. I saw the Puerto Rican young lady, who seemed so happy to see me. I even saw the young lady who played Ruth in the production. She sat like a dancer, with her back perfectly aligned. She smiled when we made eye contact. The class was full, and the discussion was lively. I looked around, taking it all in.

I challenged myself to express my opinion because I felt strongly about the topic being discussed. *"Do it Chara! Say something!"* Suddenly, I heard myself talking. The class responded as if I had been a part of their group the whole time. We all *vibed* with one another. It was a good feeling—a special feeling, another feeling of happiness.

But something changed as the class came to an end. The leader invited us all to the sanctuary for service after class, and I initially planned to go. But while sitting there, I started to doubt my decision to go in. I started to remember how I looked. My breakout was small, but by this time in my life, even the smallest breakout seemed extreme. I didn't realize at that time that I had developed body dysmorphic disorder, a condition that caused me to see my imperfections as more exaggerated than they really were. To me, others looked picture-perfect, while I looked like a monster, even when I wasn't experiencing lesions on my face. I had a pattern of thinking negatively about myself, and those thought patterns didn't leave overnight. In that short moment as class was ending, I began feeling inadequate and insecure all over again. It was simply out of habit, because I had no logical reason to feel that way. I was so used to beating myself up and feeling inadequate that I talked myself out of going into the main service when class ended. I wanted to hide. It was what I was accustomed to.

My vision of myself screamed, "Ugly and out of place!" Many thoughts started racing through my head—some race related, some out of insecurity: "They don't accept you. Why are you here? You look crazy! You don't even accept yourself, so why should they? Girl, you see how perfect these girls look? Rich and skinny... Girl, bye! Get out of here and get to your secret place." Unfortunately, in that moment, my thoughts won—again. I started walking to my car in a hurry when class ended, as others started walking to the main sanctuary.

Insecurity is a stronghold that won't allow you to easily

move forward. It is a mind-set that can cause you to run from challenges, hide from opportunities, and *remove* yourself from liberating experiences. It can cause you to only think of the negative possibilities, even in the midst of positive encounters. What's on the other side of a person's insecurity? Something called *living*. I thank God that even though I reached the car, a beautiful person, who is still in my life today, would not allow me to leave.

Two White Girls and a Puerto Rican

Just as I was getting in the car, I heard someone yelling, "Heyyyy! Heyyyy! Chara!" This person was calling out my name —literally screaming out my name—and waving. She stood at a distance at the door of the church. "Where are you going? I have a seat for you! Get back up here!" She was talking to *me*, like she knew I didn't have anywhere to go. It was like she knew I was running, getting ready to go back into my hiding place. Still standing at my car door, I saw her start to walk toward me. I got a little scared, so I opened my door a bit more just in case I needed to jump in and make a run for it. As she approached, I recognized her: she was one of the young adults from class. She wore a colorful scarf around her neck, matched with a beautiful smile. I remembered how I'd added to her comments in class. She was so sweet and genuine. We'd had the same viewpoint during the discussion, and she'd smiled at me when I agreed with her.

"I was hoping that you would stay for service," she said, "because I saved you a seat. Do you need to be somewhere? It's Sunday! Service is about to start, and I wanted to introduce you to others." I had nowhere to be. I couldn't even answer her. I just smiled, shut the car door, and said, "Okay." We walked back to the church together.

"I'm Leslie by the way."

"Hi, Leslie. Thank you."

I'm pretty sure Leslie didn't understand the depth of my

thank-you. As a matter of fact, *I* didn't even understand the depth of my thank-you. I just knew that she'd saved me from returning to my hiding place. God used her, and a couple more individuals she would introduce me that day, to push me out of the hiding place I was so accustomed to, day in and day out.

Church was good—emotionally moving and informative. After church, Leslie introduced me to her closest friends, Christina (the star dancer who played Ruth in the production) and Madel (the Puerto Rican lady I first met at the production). Leslie asked if they could take me to lunch after church. I was thrilled. I had no other plans, so I happily agreed.

They told me to meet them at a Mexican restaurant down the street from the church. The area was quite foreign to me. I was on a new side of town, an exclusive and wealthy area that I had never witnessed, although I only lived fifteen miles away. When I made it to the restaurant, Christina, Leslie, Madel, and I talked and talked. It seemed as if they were intrigued by me and were excited about getting to know me. It was so much fun. We had a lot in common, yet we were also all very different. I felt like I had known them all my life. We sat at the restaurant for hours. Before we departed, we planned to hang out the very next day, and again that following week.

We quickly became inseparable. We talked, laughed, ate together, and discussed God and ideologies. Leslie, Christina, and Madel had already been friends for a while but embraced me as if I were part of their tribe from the start. I couldn't believe it! "Look at me," I said to myself in the mirror. "I'm living! I have friends! I'm going out!" And it felt good. It felt really good. We planned to hang out with each other every chance we got. The relationships I had with them were quite different from any others I'd ever had. And we never hung out just to kill time. Each outing was intentional and fed a piece of my soul that I never even knew needed healing. My relationship with them was different because *they* were different. And because of the season I was in, I took notice.

They had a different focus and lifestyle. Their hearts were

pleasant. They wanted to make sure every decision they made aligned with their faith. Every decision! At first, I thought it was weird, but then I realized how serious they were about their faith. They didn't waste time watching, listening to, or doing anything that could possibly cause distractions in their lives. They were focused on being their best selves.

When we were together, we didn't discuss superficial things. We would discuss our life's mission and purpose. They had no idea I was struggling with deep insecurities. When I was around them, my mental battles often dissipated because they ignited my dreams as they spoke of their own. I fell in love with their mind-sets. I fell in love with their presence.

Leslie, a youth minister, was planning to become a missionary in India. Every time Leslie spoke, you could hear and feel that she genuinely cared about people. She talked with so much passion, and she showed empathy through her everyday actions. She would ask a stranger if he or she was okay, stopping to pray for them in any setting if they needed it.

Christina was part of an elite ballet company that traveled around the world ministering the gospel of Jesus Christ through dance. She traveled through parts of the world where being a Christian wasn't popular and told stories of miracles that happened in third-world countries she'd visited. We all made a point to be together when she was in town.

Madel was a computer engineer at the time and was preparing to become a missionary overseas as well. Her heart was —and still is—humongous. She would give her last dollar just to help others in need, and many times she did. Some days, I thought she was crazy for the sacrifices she made for others. But that was just Madel. A true loving soul.

Culturally, they were so different from me, but I loved it. They ate different foods, went to different places, and even watched movies that were way different from the ones I watched. One day, we all discussed going to the movies after work. We met up for dinner to discuss what we would see. I asked about the options they'd chosen, and my reaction shocked them; my normal wasn't their normal.

"What? *8 Below*? What is that about? Snow dogs? Uhhh... no! Christina, Leslie, Madel, there is no way I'm about to sit in a two-hour movie to watch dogs on screen in the snow. Do the dogs even talk?"

Madel always placed her dogs outside or in another room when I came over to her house because I wasn't comfortable around them. My new friends convinced me I would absolutely love this movie. I compromised with an expression of "yeah, right." I had no intention of enjoying the movie and thought to myself that I would take a good nap during it. Well, I was wrong, and they were so right. I walked out of that movie crying. I totally enjoyed it from beginning to end, and I couldn't believe it.

My friends still didn't know of the nonexistent life I'd led before them, because all of that changed when I met them. A famous preacher once said, "Show me your friends, and I'll show you your future." I now believe that who you hang around, mingle with, and invest your time in, can and will affect you. The people you are closest to can fuel your insecurities or cause them to diminish. And when insecurities are diminished, self-assurance develops. I couldn't help but grow because I was surrounded by young adults who were growing.

The time came when I finally shared with them about my insecurities. We were friends for around a year before I really opened up to them. I'd had good days when I didn't have a negative self-perception, but there were also days when I'd needed help—and yet never sought it from them. So, during dinner one evening, I shared with my friends my struggle with my negative self-perception. They'd seen my acne issues but never knew how much it bothered me. I cried with them, sharing my deepest desire for God to heal me, and more than anything, to reveal to me why I was still struggling with my skin after so long. They listened, inspired me with words of wisdom, and prayed with me. I told them about how my insecurities were affecting my work life, purpose, and calling. I should've known their efforts to make sure I was okay wouldn't end that day.

More than a Movie

It started as a typical night with my friends. To this day, I'm not sure if they plotted to help me see what they saw in me, or if what happened was simply God working through them.

"Hey, Chara we're planning a sleepover at Madel's house this weekend. Don't worry, she will have the dogs in another room. You in?" Leslie asked.

"You know it! Is Christina in town yet?"

"Yep! She's planning the sleep over."

It was a no-brainer. When Christina came back from traveling, we gathered. We gathered even when she was out of town, but there was never a time she was in town that we didn't gather.

Madel's house was very spacious. It made me feel as if we were locked away in a beautiful modern cabin. Hazelnut wood surround the exterior and interior of her home, even the kitchen. I absolutely loved walking on her polished hardwood floors with my shoes off. We often chilled, each with blankets, in her living room by her fireplace. She had comfortable furniture, with space to put up our feet or to lay down our heads. Her large television screen was mounted up on a wall, making us feel like we were at the movies. After we ate in the kitchen together that night, we all headed toward our gathering spot by the fireplace. Leslie made an announcement that I assumed was only for my benefit, because they were all looking at me and not at her as she talked.

"Okay, Chara, there is a movie we want to introduce to you. It's really a trilogy. The fourth one is coming out next week, and we want you to be up to speed when we go see it."

"Oh goodness Lez ... is this about more dogs?"

They laughed, and Christina said, "Well, we kinda know that you will love it." I rarely watched anything to waste time. I watched things on purpose—to motivate me, inspire me, or educate me, just like them. Avoiding TV had become my norm.

"Chris, just tell me the name of the movie, geesh!"

"Okay... It's called *X-Men*."

"It's called what? Girl I don't... I can't. Do y'all like really want me to watch three movies called *X-Men*?"

Madel spoke up. "Chara, it's really good, my friend. You will thank us later. Just watch the first one. We know you. You will love it."

Madel proceeded to put in the first movie.

I'm not sure if they enjoyed watching me or the movie more. But I got so hype by watching the first movie. It was good! I was pumped. They truly knew me. By the end of the movie, I'd analyzed the entire theme and related it to my life.

"Okay, okay, okay... this right here is deep. Okay, see we are like the mutants; we have special powers—gifts and talents—that God had given us." I was animated, and in true Chara fashion, I was up, pacing the floor, talking loudly, and expressing my thoughts.

"Put in the second one, Madel. I'm ready! Let's see how they use their powers and how they defeat their enemies."

They laughed and were thrilled that I loved the movie. By the time the second ended, they were all knocked out, asleep. But I was up! It was 2:40 a.m., and I needed to see the third film, *The Last Stand*. So I put the movie in myself, sat back, and finished the entire trilogy. At 4:40 a.m., I sat on the couch in silence. It hit me. Did my friends just set me up? Did they know this moment would have me thinking?

I took a deep look at myself. For so long, I had stopped seeing my gifts and talents because of how I felt I looked. My appearance became my focus, rather than my purpose or what I was called to do. I thought about being in the classroom when I had the most hideous breakouts and how my students still listened. My gifts were given to me not *for me*, but *for others*, and hiding behind my insecurities allowed my enemies to win.

Tears flowed from my face as I looked at my friends sleeping. I thanked God for them. They knew I would finally see and come to myself, and they used any and every avenue to help me get there. I sat there on the couch, thinking of my worth and the gifts that God had given me. Ideas started to come to me about how to make my classes and presentations fun again, how to see and seize my opportunities even as I visited the juvenile prisons. I thought about how being someone different and special is really okay, even if at times I looked like a mutant in my eyes. I stayed up staring at my friends, amazed at how God had used them. Our love for *X-Men* grew, and we talked about it all the time, naming our special powers and challenging ourselves to use them to the fullest, with wisdom.

Ready to Fly

I knew our season of kicking it would come to an end. Dreamers never just dream; reality awakens them. And reality came. Leslie moved to India as a missionary. Christina was not just one of the main dancers in the dance company; she was promoted to creative director. She traveled the world. Madel also became a missionary, traveling to South Africa and other places for her work. As for me, I would soon start on my mission to be excellent in every opportunity given me, and I would start engaging in my passions again—even my theatrical passions.

Before our season of hanging together ended, my birthday weekend rolled around, and my friends came over for dinner, along with family members, including my cousin Renata and her mom, Aunt Brenda. It was fun allowing my family to get to know my friends who were totally different from me yet alike. When everyone headed home, my three friends stayed behind, and we laughed and talked some more. Before they left, they announced that they had a gift for me. I expected to see them go to the car or reach in their purses; I didn't see any wrapped gifts ready to be given to me. Instead, we all stood, and they surrounded me in a circle. "We want to pray for you and to speak a blessing over you," Leslie said. They each placed their hands on me, and asked God to heal me from the inside out. They prayed for peace in my apartment, asked God to open my eyes to see His will for my life, and rebuked depression, sickness, and sadness from me. They declared that I would reach the world with every gift and talent God had placed in me for His glory. My friends gave me the greatest gift of all; they ignited my faith. They helped me build my trust in God, and they taught me how to live as I simply observed their lifestyle. My inner circle healed me in more ways than I can describe. The impact they had on me can't be erased. That year, I discovered just how vital relationships are, and I'm still amazed that it all started with me building my relationship first with myself, with *just Chara*.

CHAPTER 17

CALLED FOR PURPOSE

As usual, I waited for the gates of the juvenile prison to open. Three years before, I had ridden with Dr. Mae Henry to the prison, but now I was traveling by myself. No one could drive in or out of the prison unless cleared by the guards. Massive gray gates surrounded the entire mega-campus. A loud alarm buzzer would sound as the gates separated to let me drive through. That wouldn't be the first gate I'd have to get through to see the girls behind bars. Once I walked in the building, I had to place all my belongings and my program supplies in a bucket to be viewed and approved. I was then patted down and searched before fully entering the building. When I walked through any gate on the prison grounds, big or small, the gates would lock behind me, resounding with a loud clicking and reminding me I was not headed to an informal gathering with a typical group of girls. This was prison.

I had planned for this meeting to be different from past sessions I had conducted at the prison. I was prepared, excited about my lesson, and ready to start fresh. Hanging with my friends had helped change my perception about this job. I realized I was created to solve problems using my gifts and talents—my own superpowers.

I didn't know it yet, but one prisoner in particular was about to have a profound impact on me, reminding me to never,

ever doubt my gifts or my purpose on earth. I was getting ready to not only understand true beauty but to experience it on a greater level than ever before.

One of the female guards approached me after I was checked in and cleared to proceed. She was new and seemed to be the only guard excited about her job. With a smile on her face she asked, "Ms. Chara, are you ready for me to escort you to your room?"

"How many girls do you think I will have today?" I asked.

"Ma'am, I don't know what is happening to our young females, but they are coming into this prison like flies. I know you normally have about twenty to twenty-five girls in class, but today you have about forty-two girls."

"Wowsers!" I stated. "Well, I'm ready when you are."

The new guard made my return seem even more meaningful and purposeful. She took her job seriously, and it showed. She informed me that the guards who were escorting the girls to my room were now required to stay with me at all times. I knew that the guards should stay with the girls throughout programming; however, some guards who knew me well would consider my class their break time. They were aware that I could handle the girls in my class, especially once the lessons started. They had witnessed my firmness toward the girls when needed, and they knew the girls wouldn't get bored sitting in the class with me. They would be too busy engaging in and anticipating the lesson to start drama. After all, many of the girls were like little kids. They often forgot about their hard personas when they were in the midst of winning games and prizes. They got excited about receiving stickers and candy, and cheered for their teammates as if they were on an actual game show. Truth be told, many of the girls had missed out on having a real childhood. During my lessons, the little girl in them would show up inside the body of a teenager incarcerated in a juvenile prison.

The room I was assigned to this time (their recreational room) was quite large and bare. Chairs were in the room only because I requested them. The large brick walls were covered in crusted, peeling green and yellow paint. Bright lights flickered, magnifying the decaying walls. The hallways looked the same as the rooms. What I hated the most was that the entire building yielded an echo because of the extremely high ceilings.

I could hear the girls talking and walking as they approached the room, accompanied by the sound of keys dangling from the side pockets of the guards. I was a bit nervous because this was a new group. It was as if it was my first time entering the prison. For various reasons, not all the girls in the prison could attend the program. I assumed that it depended on the crimes committed or the girls' level of maturity; I never really knew. I waited patiently as the girls turned the corner to walk into my room. They were getting closer. "Should I peep my head out," I thought?

Suddenly, before I could do so, screams erupted. I first heard an ugly cry. I would later learn that a young girl on her way to my lesson had just unexpectedly but intentionally been hit hard from behind. The shouts of more girls echoed so loudly that it startled me. I could hear the sounds of pushing, shoving, the sound of shoes scuffing the floor, cries, and punches all at the same time. Some girls yelled, "Fight, Fight!" Other girls were screaming, "She's stomping her, she's stomping her!" Yet some others were hollering, "Beat her!" Profanity laced words filled the air from *both* the girls and the guards. By the time I walked out into the hallway, what I saw horrified me. I saw girls wrestling one another, punching each other, and guards grabbing many of them and pushing them off each other; they were clearly struggling to regain control of the group but ultimately were powerless to quell the violence. I had never witnessed a group of girls so out of control while at the prison. I stood there, shocked and bewildered at what was happening before my eyes. This group was quite different, and it was painfully obvious.

The guards finally regained some sense of order and control of the situation after a disturbingly long time. It was apparent who the ringleader of the brawl was, so the fatigue-clad female guards angrily surrounded her, cursing at her while attempting to restrain her. It looked like a scene from a military boot camp. They mocked her and vented their frustrations on her using offensive and brutal words. They declared to her that she was a piece of trash and that she would never leave the facility because of her behavior. Frowning with a face full of rage, the young prisoner stood still, fist balled up, and looked each guard up and down as if she was waiting for them to break the rules and touch her without cause. The new guard seemingly unaware or unphased by what had just taken place interrupted in a quiet yet soothing manner: "Okay, you guys, can the girls still have class with Ms. Chara, or is class cancelled?" No one said a thing. The atmosphere was tense. The girls watched the guards pacing back and forth in anger and out of breath. One guard finally announced to the girls in a loud voice, "If you even *look* at another girl in the wrong way, I will cancel this class, and you will not come out of your cells for the *entire* weekend. DO YOU UNDERSTAND ME? Now MOVE!"

The girls formed a line and walked into the recreation room. I stood in silence standing by the door. The young lady who had started the fight was outside with the newest guard, pleading her case as she wiped off a small amount of blood from her lip. I didn't want to start class yet unless I knew she was coming. Because the rest of the guards were in the room with the girls, I stepped back out into the hallway and overheard the young lady begging not to go back to solitary confinement. She wanted to be given another chance. She exclaimed, "You know I was just trying to defend myself. You know that. I put that on everything!" She then looked at me and said she wanted to stay in my class to see what it was all about. Another guard came outside, and she wasn't listening to her at all. But because I'd put in so much work to prepare for a fun class, I stood up for her and asked the guards to allow her to return. The new guard announced that she would bring the young lady back to class once she visited the nurse's office to get her wounds treated.

When I stepped back into the class, I introduced myself to the girls and explained the purpose of the class. I even addressed the fight, expressing my disappointment and my expectations. They all seemed to have listened and verbally agreed to be on their best behaviors. We talked for a little while about what happened and the importance of respecting each other. But, before I officially started the lesson, the guards brought back the so-called troublemaker.

"Oh, welcome back!" I said.

"Ms. Chara," the guard announced, "this is Chrissy, and she will be on her best behavior."

"What? My name ain't no d*$% Chrissy. Don't play with me. Man, my new name is Christopher." Looking at the class, "Ain't that right y'all?"

Chrissy wanted to be called Christopher or Chris at all times. She wore cornrows in her head and carried herself with a masculine persona. She was a very beautiful girl. Her caramel skin tone was super smooth—not one single blemish in sight. She had strong facial bone features that illuminated her smile, which could light up the room, just as her frown could darken it. She had perfect whitened teeth that flashed when she talked. Her dogmatic male persona became evident when she talked or even whispered to her female peers. Extra guards stayed in the room because of her. I felt as if it was my job now to show them Chrissy could participate without causing problems.

I set up a big white paper board, propped up by an easel and introduced my version of "Win, Lose, or Draw," taken from the traditional game. The girls split up into teams and had to draw movie themes, nursery rhymes, songs, or popular phrases. The game was hilarious, as each team tried their best to guess what their artist was sketching. Even the guards started laughing and chiming in on what should have been drawn to get the point across. At first Chrissy slumped down in her chair, observing the crowd without saying a word. Even though she was a part of a group, she didn't participate. When the time came to call up another person to draw, I suggested to the team that Chrissy should do it. She looked at me as if I had disrespected her. The girls in the room seemed either afraid or at least respectful of her. But one thing was clear: most of the guards hated her.

"Come on, Chrissy" I said.

"What I tell you? My name is Christopher—or you can call me Chris," she blurted out.

I sensed that, like every tough girl, Chrissy was about to test me. She got up and started walking around me, proceeding to flirt. Looking me up and down, she said, "But d*$% you can call me anything you want to, shorty. I like you."

I quickly had to show Chrissy that I was not someone she could disrespect, and I had to do it fast because the guards were already at the edge of their seats, ready to pounce.

"First, my name is *Ms*. Chara. Second, what you are doing now is quite disrespectful, and I know that you know better than that. You know what is appropriate and what is not. So why would you stand in front of your peers and act like a child? Act your age and win the game for your team."

My suspicion was right: most teens love competition, and I offered a change of focus to help her see that she had an opportunity to shine in a different way. What happened next would shock us all. "A'ight, A'ight ... I see you. I got you. Let me have the pen and watch me win. And oh, only *you* can call me Chrissy. Got it? I'm ready now."

Chrissy was quite the competitor. She took the game seriously and won every round for her team. Her team decided they wanted her to stay at the front as their designated drawer. It was a close competition, and the girls were all excited during the game. Chrissy's team took the prize, and boy, were they excited. Right when they won the last round, they jumped up like little kids, screaming ecstatically, hugging and high-fiving each other. Surprisingly, you could even see the guards smirking. It was beautiful to see Chrissy move from not participating to winning the game for her team.

As always, once the game portion was finished, it was reflection time. I asked, "How many of you were trying to guess what was being drawn on the board, but it looked unfamiliar, crazy, or just plain weird? When did the drawings become clearer?" Out of all people, Chrissy—the troublemaker—was the main one who screamed out the answer: "The messages became clearer as the person kept drawing, and just like in life, we should keep going even when life is blurry or seems bleak."

I was stunned. We were all shocked. Chrissy related my message to the group before I could. I broke the silence and exclaimed, "Exactly, Chrissy!" I proceeded to engage her in conversation in front of everyone. Her peers seemed surprised she was taking the discussion part of the lesson seriously. She had an extreme impact on the atmosphere during the discussion component. Her perspective on the lesson was delightful. I applauded her answers, and we discussed what to do when life doesn't seem clear and how to draw out a clearer picture to their future. Others chimed in and gave their opinion. Many shared their personal experiences, and the segment ended with the girls encouraging each other.

Chrissy told me she enjoyed class and would try her best to stay out of confinement so she could attend the next one. The guards overheard our conversation and literally blurted out. "Yeah right, Chrissy! You'll be back in solitary confinement before the day is over." Turning away from the guards toward me, Chrissy said, "You see what I'm talking 'bout? They could care less about me. They want us all to lose. Anyway, Ms. Chara, I'll see you next week." I was really hoping she would use the skills she learned in class so I could see her again. I thought about her all that week as I prepared for the next class period to roll around.

Gifted

I believed in Chrissy and really wanted to see her in class. But on the next visit, when I walked into the prison, the guards didn't even give me a chance to ask. They blurted, "Yo' girl didn't make it. She's in SC" (solidarity confinement). When I walked in the class, the girls let me know too: "Chrissy didn't make it. She was fighting again." However, the girls passed on a message: "Chrissy wanted us to tell you not to give up on her and that she'll be here next class period. She just f*%$#@ up but will keep going as you taught her to."

I smiled and gave them a message to send back to her. One thing I noticed was that Chrissy had a gift that even she couldn't see. The girls followed her, even if she wasn't in their presence. They were more serious about the class because she was serious. She instructed them to tell her everything about the class when she got out, so they paid attention and were, ironically, on their best behavior.

My next class with the girls would be the next month. Many of the girls had served their time and were being released. I wanted to make sure I gave each class what they could use for life. I realized my job was an opportunity to make lasting changes in their lives, just from one class period. And I always looked forward to seeing the girls during my scheduled hours.

My skin issues had continued off and on. On this day, I had a breakout, but I knew I could not allow my imperfections to stop me from going to the prison. For the first time ever, I wasn't concerned about how I looked. I was focused on seeing the girls. After all, two to three weeks had passed since my last visit.

When I arrived, the first guard who saw me smiled, "Well, well, well, guess who is in class waiting on you? She did it. She shocked us all." When I walked in the room, Chrissy smiled at me, and I couldn't help but smile really hard right back at her. I hugged her and acknowledged her accomplishment, asking her to help me as I led class. I had prepared a special lesson just for her. I wasn't sure if she was still there, but with the way her behavior had been, I figured she would be there for a while. I wanted all the girls to really understand their worth and value before leaving, as I too was learning even more to discover mine. I didn't tell Chrissy the lesson was prepared especially for her. I just prayed that she would be impacted by it.

Thank You, Ms. Chara

I was escorted for this class period to a different setting—the campus chapel. The recreational rooms were finally getting an overdue paint job. The chapel was pretty small but very comfortable. The ceilings were lower, so there was no resounding echo. Red pews filled the sanctuary, and there was an elevated stage close to the pews so all could see. This time, I had fifty-plus girls in class with me. The word had spread around the prison that my class was fun, exciting, and edifying. Even the guards told me that my class was now a part of their award system to entice the girls to behave correctly.

I always had a game that matched my lessons, and the girls expected it. I knew Chrissy enjoyed basketball and bragged about her skills often. This game was similar to basketball, but with a twist. We used two small laundry baskets and two soft-grip pink basketballs. The object of the game was that the person holding the basket would move it every time a person from the opposing team tried to shoot the ball. The goal was to make it hard to score a basket.

Chrissy got in position, ready to shoot, unaware that the baskets would move as soon as she tried to make the basket. She frowned after her first shot didn't go in, and the crowd shouted in laughter. She exclaimed, "Wait, that's not fair! The basket moved." I encouraged her to continue—no matter what, to try to do her best to win a point. The game was obviously hard for her and others. Some teams complained and literally gave up. They yelled, "As long as the baskets kept moving, there's no reason to try." I didn't correct them because the point was to see their endurance. I was waiting to see their reactions. Some girls didn't even go up to the stage to try because they felt the game was either unfair or impossible to beat. They stood behind the pews, screaming for the others.

But something happened as Chrissy was playing—and I knew it would. Chrissy became determined to win, despite the challenge. Each team could rotate shooters, but the line of rotating shooters became smaller and smaller, because many went to sit down in the pews, giving up on the game. On Chrissy's team, she was now the only shooter. Once the ball would bounce off the basket or simply air-drop from missing the basket, she would run to grab her ball, stand back behind her line, and shoot again. After a while, the team Chrissy was competing with simply gave up, and the only people left on the stage were Chrissy and the person moving the basket. They were both out of breath and sweating, as Chrissy would not allow the person moving the basket to rest; she just kept shooting. This went on and on for a while, and the crowd all started to cheer her on. As screams from the pews continued, it seemed to fuel Chrissy to keep trying. She picked up the ball, and every time she shot it, it would almost go in; she was outthinking the mover of the basket and fake shooting in one direction but then actually shooting in another.

I jumped onstage. Chrissy was breathing hard and frowning. I asked the audience, particularly the participants who gave up, "What's happening here? What do you see in Chrissy?" One shouted, "Chrissy is determined, even though she ain't gon' win." Others shouted, "Chrissy is still playing, even though it's hard for her to make the shot." With that comment, Chrissy then slammed the ball in between her hands, screaming, "I'm a beast! I got this!" For some reason, this got the crowd hype. Their negatives turned into positives: "Come on Chrissy! You got this!" And the game continued.

She was once again unsuccessful at making a shot, due to the movement of the basket. I challenged Chrissy with a question: "Chris, what are you going to do differently, since you are having a hard time making your goal?" She was clearly getting upset. "What are you going to do, Chrissy? Will you give up, or will you reach your goal?" I began to talk to the audience as she played against the person moving the basket. "This is no longer about a game of basketball; this is about the game of life. Every time you try to make one step, it seems like everything falls apart, and you can't reach your goal. *What will you do differently?*"

Chrissy started screaming, pacing, and thinking.

I took advantage of the moment. "Life will make you feel like you can't make it when you get out of here," I said, "but you have to be determined, *be strategic*, and be smart. Chrissy, how will you reach your goal? Think. You must do something differently!" She paused. She stopped shooting and held the ball in one hand. Then, suddenly she marched up to the person holding the basket, screaming, "Ahhhhhh!" and forcefully put her ball inside. Everyone went crazy with cheers. Chrissy realized that no one told her she had to shoot the goal; she just had to make it into the basket to win the point. She was out of breath and looked tired, but she had given it her all. Then I saw this masculine persona do something that none of us were expecting. She started crying.

She stood by me onstage, as all the other ladies now stood together in front of the first pew watching us. It was reflection time, and somehow, we all felt Chrissy's emotions. I told the girls, "When you leave here, you can continue down the same path in hopes of something changing, or you can *be* different and *do* something different for a change. Many will keep their same patterns, but you—you—know better now, and you must do better, because your old habits aren't working." As I related the game to the message more and more, the girls listened, and because many saw Chrissy in tears, wiping her face, they, too, became teary-eyed. I acknowledged Chrissy and applauded her in front of the others for not giving up. As she looked me in the eye, I encouraged her to take that same type of determination that she had in a game and apply it to her real game of life.

I didn't want to bring too much more attention to Chrissy; I knew she was tired of her old habits and ready for a change. I knew that *that* moment was more than a game for her. I looked up and saw the guards, who had been standing outside the chapel, enter the room. "Let's huddle," I announced. Chrissy and I stepped down from the stage to join the girls as each placed their arms around the others, forming a large circle. I asked, "Chrissy, are you ok?"

I will never forget her expression. She exclaimed, "It's like... it's like... I get it. I get it now. I want to win in life like I was trying to win in basketball. I want to get out of here and never return." The girls applauded Chrissy and each other. We all hugged, and they were escorted out.

As class ended, my heart melted in joy. I had just witnessed my small idea of a game bring change to a young crowd. My superpower had been utilized in a mighty way. As I packed up my belongings, suddenly the glass door opened again. Chrissy had asked the guards if she could run back to me before I left. She walked up to me and said, "Thank you, Ms. Chara." I smiled, hugged her, and told her I was proud of her. What she didn't know was that I was also proud of me.

When I returned to the prison weeks later, I was told Chrissy had been released. I was honored that God allowed me to use my gifts and talents to help her and many of the other girls. I have no idea where she is today or how she is doing, but what I do know is that she received the skills needed to succeed. Did she use them? I'm not sure, but I was able to at least offer them to her and impact her. Using *my* gifts, talents and abilities showed me what mattered. As usual in that season, I continued to break out and didn't want to leave the house. But what God had placed in me to do seemed more important than waiting on a bump to go down from my face. Using my inner abilities caused me to *glow* and *grow* in a way that was unexplainable. That day while driving home, I fell out of love with how I looked and in love with who I was becoming.

CHAPTER 18

THE POWER OF BEING ME

Wearing four-inch heels, skinny-leg jeans, and a white blazer, I walked in a room full of college football players to give a creative lesson on sexual harassment. Dr. Mae Henry was with me. She invited me to speak with her at a highly respected college in Mississippi—to their athletics department. Whistles and flirty comments flew freely as I set up the room, but during the presentation time, the players were quiet and listened as we spoke. By the end of the session, one football player stood up and thanked us for coming, because he had no idea his actions were borderline inappropriate; the information given was just what he needed to hear. He didn't want to make any dumb decisions that would prevent him from getting into the NFL. It felt good to hear the feedback. As we proceeded to pack up and leave, the coaches sent the players to their next segment. They had a full weekend of lessons and lectures. I was honored to be part of their journey. I had been using my superpowers more often and focusing less on my skin.

On our way out of the room, some coaches stayed behind to help us pack our things. They were all nice-looking, visibly in shape, charming guys. One of the coaches walked me to my car and asked me for my number. He was tall and very handsome. He asked if he could take me out to dinner to get to know me more. I was shocked and caught off guard. "Who, me?" I asked.

"Yeah, you," he said. "Could I take you out?"

Dating a guy in my condition was something I just couldn't fathom. I had gotten to a place where I enjoyed living my life with just being me and taking the steps to accept me, to the point that I didn't think of allowing the opposite sex into my world. I didn't even have the clearest skin that day, and because my focus was on work, I had forgotten about my face. But for some reason, when he asked to take me out, I remembered. I quickly declined the coach's offer but thanked him for asking. Truth is, I was afraid if we started dating, he would eventually leave me because I wasn't perfect. It happened in college over hair, so why in the world would he like me with the imperfections in my skin?

I was shocked that someone was attracted to me—up close. It was new to me. But I closed the door mentally by saying, "Note to self: Love on Chara… just Chara, accept Chara, date Chara, because no one can love you, Chara, like you." There was no way in the world a guy could come into my life and like me as is—or could he?

My next destination was my cousin Renata's house. By this season of my life, I regularly relaxed with her and my aunt. We watched encouraging programming, just as I did with my other friends. Renata played a vital part in my life at that time. She was the first family member I felt comfortable being around when my face broke out. Well, truthfully, I never felt *comfortable*, because her skin was flawless, but she pushed me not to fall back into my lonely shell when I was far from perfection. She would call and say, "You on your way over here, right?" I would just laugh, make a U-turn from going home, and go hang out with her. She embraced me and spoke so many encouraging words over me all the time, especially when my face broke out. Her energy gave me hope, and their house made me feel so happy and welcomed. They became a safe haven for me when the season with Madel, Christina, Leslie, and me changed.

Renata and I chilled with the big-screen TV in the living room, flipping channels, laughing, screaming, and joking. I'm not sure why the TV was even on; we never closed our mouths to hear anything. But one night, while we flipped through the channels, we came upon Donnie McClurkin, a gospel singer who was preaching. We didn't know he was a preacher; we only knew him as a singer. Renata stopped flipping the channels and turned up the volume to hear a little bit of his sermon. "God wants to bless you in what you feel like is the worst season of your life," he said. "Now, imagine that blessing. What does it look like?" I laughed aloud and said to my cousin, "Girl, that's like God allowing me to get married in this season of my life, with this dumb skin issue. It's like a guy actually saying he wants to marry me, and I'm not perfect yet." I laughed and laughed more. She wasn't necessarily laughing, and I guess God wasn't laughing either, because what transpired next in my life blew my mind.

But GOD

It was one of those days. I had a *bad* breakout. But I promised my mom I would join a ministry called Crossroads, a new singing group/worship service that gathered often. I told my Aunt Trice I had big plans to join a group but was nervous as to how I would be treated, looked at, and examined. She encouraged me to put on my stilettos, comb my hair, get to that group, and exude "Chara." I smiled, laughed, and as always, by that time, encouraged myself to be myself, despite what was going on with me on the outside. This was another level of growth for me. It wasn't easy, but it was my mission to be me, despite how I looked on the outside.

I arrived at the group's rehearsal, held at the leader's house. I totally enjoyed myself. No one was even thinking or caring about my skin. I saw familiar faces, and new ones, such as the keyboardist who barely looked up while playing keys. He was in his own world. The atmosphere was inviting and exciting. I even grabbed a solo.

Singing background felt refreshing. I hadn't done it in years, since I was a teenager. At the end of the rehearsal, the leader—a pastor who became a mentor to me—announced that he believed in fellowshipping with one another. He invited us to go out to eat. "I will pay for everyone's dinner," he said. I debated if I should go. A free dinner sounded good, but it would mean I would have to sit with people who could analyze my skin.

Fighting the urge to revert to my hiding place, I pushed myself to go. There, I sat by the keyboard player; who was still in his own world. This guy was an undercover comedian. I had totally misjudged him. He had everyone in the restaurant cracking up. I thought, "Oh dear Lord, he's cracking jokes on people. He may talk about me; I got to get out of here." But he clearly wasn't focused on me or my skin. So I joined the sea of laughter and embraced the environment. It felt good.

Suddenly, when the food came out, the atmosphere became quieter.

"So, what do you do?" he asked me.

"I teach abstinence and character education to students in the school systems and even in the prisons."

"Oh so you're practicing abstinence? Well, there's no need for me to talk to you, then," he said.

The people sitting on his left and right started laughing. He proceeded to make more jokes toward me. I had no chance to joke back, because he had the whole room laughing. I braced myself for an insensitive joke about my skin, but it never came. Even so, after the 750th joke he made on me, I called him "the devil" to his face. Apparently, that got to him, because he stopped making jokes and throughout dinner reminded me that I called him the devil. "I can't believe you called me the devil. I'm appalled." When dinner was over, he, along with another woman, walked me to my car. He repeated himself: "You called me the devil. How could you?" I apologized, and we laughed.

We then started a serious conversation about life. We all discussed love, finances, and kids. Two hours later, the restaurant had closed, and the three of us were still in the parking lot, talking. He was so intriguing. His gift of wisdom was paramount and caused me to change my perspective on several issues that I was very adamant about. Even though we didn't exchange numbers that night, I was okay with that, because, after all, I had a big breakout. I didn't expect him to like me, and a part of me didn't want him to. But I couldn't stop thinking about him when I got home. His conversation illuminated my thinking. I knew there was something special about him, and I wanted him in my life. Not as a boyfriend or anything like that, but as a friend. So I prayed, asking God to bless me with this guy as a platonic friend. For the first time ever, I'd felt comfortable talking to a guy without being consumed about my image. Our entire three-hour conversation was on another level. But never did I think that this friendship could evolve into more.

More than a Friend

Because my friends were not around as much, I decided to go back to my home church. The Sunday I walked in, guess who was sitting at the piano? Yes, the guy that I had met at the singing ministry! The guy I'd called a devil while eating dinner. Now, my home church wasn't—and still isn't—a small church, so I was very shocked to see him as one of the musicians. After the service, I approached him.

"What are you doing here?" I asked.

He replied, "I just took a job here. Why are you stalking me?"

I laughed and burst his bubble by telling him I'd gone to the church since I was a kid. I congratulated him on the new job, and he thanked me. "See you later at rehearsal," we said.

I saw him the next week at the Crossroads ministry rehearsal, and we talked some more. Nothing serious. I expressed my love for the arts, and he invited me to his studio to hear the music he was working on. There, we talked more. My prayer was coming to fruition. We were becoming friends. Now, again he didn't seem interested in me, but I was totally okay with that; I didn't expect him to like me romantically.

He found out about my past involvement with the arts at church and challenged me to partner with him at my home church to do a musical production. I took the challenge, but not without inviting him to a ballet production my friend Christina was involved in. To my surprise he agreed to go with me. My cousin Renata said, "Uhhh... he likes you. Girl, he's going to a ballet with you." I never thought twice. I saw it as scouting other productions together before creating our own.

The more we worked on our project, the more we got to know one another. This project was no small feat. The church we both attended, my home church, had a full performing arts ministry of dancers, singers, actors, musicians, and more. I wrote the production, and he was over the entire music department, adding music to fit each scene. We gathered often to make things cohesive before we presented it to the several hundred participants who would be a part of the production. Then one day, as a routine, I stopped by his studio really late to work on my piece of the production as he worked on his piece. We stayed up and talked, literally, through the night. We talked about everything you could think of. I don't remember us getting any work done that night. I just wanted to pick his brain because he seemed so young to be so full of wisdom. It was intriguing. He asked me questions as well, and I shared my world with him. Then, in one moment we looked up and suddenly noticed that it was 5 a.m.

He suggested, "Let me take you to breakfast before you go home."

"For sure!"

Believe it or not, I had a breakout that day. But he felt like such a friend that it didn't matter to me. His name was Johnathan McGill. A dark-chocolate, handsome gentlemen with a unique and brilliant mind. A self-taught skilled musician with a witty personality. A gentleman to any lady. His smile was mesmerizing. When you saw him talking to any woman, his age or older, it never failed—he made her laugh or smile. I knew everything about him—or so I thought.

A week later, I returned to his studio and found out the one thing I didn't know about him—yep, he had a girlfriend. He said they were taking a break, to see where things would lead them. I was disappointed, but I wasn't mad. I kept telling myself and everybody else that we were just friends. I was so content with being by myself, loving my work, and challenging me to get to know me daily that being sure not to lose his friendship was all I cared about in the end. The day he told me about his girlfriend, I told him that I should stop coming around as often, out of respect for her. "You should be spending time working things out instead of building new friendships," I said.

I was shocked at his response. He said, "There is something about you that I can't lose. You're different. Don't walk away from me just yet. Stay in my life. There's something special about you." I smiled, gave him a hug, and left.

Separation really does make the heart grow fonder. I missed my friend. I didn't go to his studio often after that, but we worked on the project together. I noticed other girls in the church were into him. He went out to lunch and dinner with some, and others also came to his studio. I was slightly jealous, so I fought more and more to remove myself from the thought of having a relationship with someone while dealing with skin issues. Besides, I was still trying to find the best skin regime to work for me.

One day, he mentioned to me that he had broken up with his girlfriend. It was a long-distance relationship that just didn't work out. We started hanging out just as friends again, and I saw that he also added more friends who were girls to his schedule too. I played it cool and continued to be me. He continued to call me often, and we continued to hang out more and more. Though I was trying my best not to develop feelings for this guy, I finally asked him one day, "What did you mean by saying I'm different... special? By this point a year had passed but I couldn't shake what he said, so I asked him. He explained that

I had a sense of confidence about myself and that every time I did something at my job, in the community, or anywhere, I did it with a sense of self-assurance and clarity, showing I knew who I was. Then he said, "I like that about you. You're beautiful. I've never met anyone like you. I like how you know you."

That night I went home knowing that our relationship was different. Something had changed. He told me he really liked me, and he called me beautiful. I had dated a couple musicians before while on meds, when everything was perfect. Yet here was this guy expressing to me that I was beautiful when I was extremely flawed. I had no magic pill to make my flaws go away. I had no magic creams that prevented breakouts. All I had was the power to be me, and that was what he liked. Had I discovered *real* beauty and put it on display? To be beautiful for so long had meant to be physically perfect, and I didn't fit that picture. I was a size 2 again because of my salad eating, but I had bad skin. But he called me beautiful. He saw something deeper.

True Love

One Mississippi fall day, I received a call from Johnathan. We had been talking often for about six months. He asked me to come to a specific park on a specific date. Not just any park, a botanical garden with lush landscaping and shaded walking paths with several sitting areas. Perfect for pictures. I marked the day on my calendar (two and a half weeks out) and prayed God would bless me with the clearest skin that day. My friend guy had one request of me; he asked me to dress up, so I bought a cute new dress.

On the week of the date, I could tell I was about to have a bad breakout. I prayed and prayed, trying not to cry and make things worse. But I couldn't help it. I cried. "God, please… not now. Not this week." I woke up the day of our very special date with a really bad breakout—a serious one. It had been awhile since I'd had inflamed lesions, but two now appeared on my face. "We need to reschedule," I told him. He knew something was up, because he knew I'd been excited about our scheduled time together.

On the day of the outing, I opened up to him and told him I was having a serious breakout, one like he hadn't seen. "I don't want to go to the park," I said. That day he promised me he could see beyond my flaws. "I just want to be with you," he said. "I planned a special day just for you." He asked me not to cancel just because I wasn't perfect. "The day will still be perfect," he said. I was scared. It would be the first time he would see me at my worst.

I arrived at the park in a black and white mod dress, with high heels—and you already know I hated dressing up when I had a breakout, but I did for him. When I arrived, the place was beautiful. He stood with two small journals in his hand, along with a camera. I almost turned around when I saw the camera, because there was no way I was going to take pictures with a major breakout. We argued about taking pictures for about thirty minutes, but he promised he would allow me to get the prints first. There were several sitting areas in the park, and in each sitting area, he placed a different theme for us to discuss (dreams, goals, family, love, career). Then, before leaving each area, we took a picture together, then wrote out prayers in our new journals about that particular theme of discussion. He wanted to grow with me; he wanted us to grow together. We became exclusive that day, sharing our deepest desires. We built more than a romantic relationship: a strong foundation for our friendship. Later we picked up something to eat to bring back to the studio to chill and talk. It ended up being a great day. My first day being with someone who *liked* me on a day I looked nowhere near perfect.

Months had passed after our special date, and our friendship continued to grow. February fifteenth rolled around, and I thought it would be just another night with my bestie. We'd planned to meet the day after Valentine's Day, due to his work schedule. He had walked with me through so much, good and bad, by this time in my life. He saw me without makeup. He visited me with acne cream all over my face. We were super close, best friends, and I trusted him.

When I walked into his studio, he said he had something for me. I got excited, expecting a card with money in it or some candy. I just knew it was a teddy bear or something with the words "Happy Valentine's Day" on it. Instead of handing me flowers, he handed me a pack of pictures. I was confused until I opened them. I screamed, "Oh my God... oh my God!

They were the pictures we took at the garden. He knew I would peruse each picture as if I were a detective, because I was so adamant about making sure I saw the photos before anyone else did. I had never taken pictures with someone before in the midst of my imperfections. I looked slowly at each photo. Then, toward the end of the prints, there was a picture I didn't recognize: a portrait of a beautiful ring in its case, with the words "WILL YOU MARRY ME?" I stared at it for the longest time, trying to figure out why it was in the stack. I turned around to ask him, only to see that he was right behind me, kneeling down and holding the exact ring that was in the picture. My best friend was asking me to marry him.

The guy who had walked with me through my worst days still wanted to marry me. The girl who was so far from perfect was actually getting married. The girl who finally found the love to love herself now found true love from someone else— the man of her dreams. I couldn't believe I was getting married.

On October 4, 2008, what Donnie McClurkin professed came true: "God wants to bless you even in what you feel like is the worst season of your life." I and my bestie got married on Tybee Island, in Savannah, Georgia. And just like many days before when I prayed for the clearest skin, God said no on that day. However, my skin never went back to extreme, inflamed lesions after my wedding day. That was the last day of my worst breakouts. Yes, scarring from the aftermath of having lesions became a struggle, but I have never had a face full of lesions after my wedding day. I guess Donnie was right! God wanted to show me something that would change me forever: God wanted to show

Trying to Get to a Place Called Pretty:How I Discovered the Trut...

me *the truth about beauty.*

CHAPTER 19

THE TRUTH ABOUT BEAUTY

B
efore when I was asked, "Who are you?" I had no clue. I couldn't even answer. Today, if you were to ask me, "Chara, who are you?" here is what I would say:

> *I am an impressive, awe-inspiring, marvelous, and compassionate individual created to change the world with every gift and talent that God has placed within me. I have a personality that causes me to be serious-minded most of the time, but I can also let my hair down and have fun. I'm often described as "animated," and I must say, I agree with that. I'm emotionally aware of my healthy and/or unhealthy feelings, and I love to explore the root causes and triggers of them all. I am equipped and skilled with creative capabilities and proficiencies that I love to use to enhance, enlighten, and educate people—especially teenagers. I am beautiful because I know who I am. I am super unique. I am truly one of a kind. I am an original being, one that exists for multiple purposes, and I know that there is no one like me. That, alone, makes me special.*

You see, I went on a journey and discovered the truth about

beauty by simply *discovering me*. In the midst of, literally, the ugliest season of my life, I found beauty—I found me.

True beauty is when you discover YOU! It has nothing to do with how you look, but it has everything to do with WHO YOU ARE.

For so long, I tried to measure up to the world's ideology of beauty, and it brought me hopelessness every single time I couldn't measure up. I look back at my life in amazement, shocked at how obsessed I was with wanting society to accept me. Shocked at how insecure and disturbed I was about my physical image. A freedom developed within me when I truly discovered me. I became content with seeing the real me and learned to accept me, flaws and all. I stop caring about the opinions of others. I stopped trying to measure up to society's definition of beauty and uncovered an inner peace, joy, happiness, and wholeness. I now refuse to live my life for the approval of others. The change that has happened is all something kind of supernatural.

I am grateful that I discovered one of the greatest gifts of all: I discovered me. I know now that real beauty has nothing to do with how I look, but it has everything to do with who I am. Because I now know me, body discontentment and dissatisfactions can no longer hinder me from progressing. Knowing myself dispelled every lie that I've heard or ever will hear against the truth of my beauty. I had to start seeing myself in a positive light and love me despite my physical imperfections. I stopped hiding in my apartment and learned to live out my life. This opened the doors for me to accept myself and love from others.

My journey continues. The truth is, discovering who you are is life changing and ongoing. Every year, every month, I grow to another level of freedom. I'm not the same Chara that I was yesterday. That's the beauty about discovering oneself. There are levels to this thing. The greater the level, the greater the freedom. Writing this book is another level of my freedom. It's a process, a beautiful journey.

The Keys to Discover You

This world is consumed by image. It always has been, and it probably always will be. But that doesn't mean you and I have to be consumed by it. We can be the examples to show what *true beauty* looks and feels like, and how to walk in its authenticity. We can be free from insecurities, body image dissatisfaction, and negative self-image. We can do that. You can do that. How, you may ask? By discovering true beauty—discovering you. *You possess a beauty that has never been seen, and there will never, ever be another person like you.* So when you walk in *who* you are destined to be, a unique beauty is displayed for the world to see and to experience. The most amazing part is, only *you* can display it.

I started my journey to freedom by discovering five foundational components to who I am, and now I want to share that message with you. You have the same five key components that make up who you are too. What are they? What must you discover?

You must discover your **social self**, your **intellectual self**, your **emotional self**, your **spiritual self**, and your **physical self**. As I reflect on how I did this, allow me to pinpoint how you can do the same.

Discovering Your Social Self

Remember when Patricks asked me, "Chara, who are you?" What was the first thing I did after he asked me that question? I sat down to write out ninety-six questions and answered each one. I interviewed me. I took the time to really get to know me socially; I discovered my persona. I came face-to-face with what I liked, what I disliked, and why.

But I didn't stop there. I challenged myself to take action based on the answers to my questions. This opened up my world to experience life, friends, and joy. I found that not everyone is cynical and caught up in the superficial things of this world. I was looking for like-minded individuals. But I would not have known where to start if I hadn't taken the time to get to know me. I got to know my *social self*.

Your *social self* is an important component of who you are. Once you discover you socially, you will begin to move differently, live differently, and appreciate *who you are*. If a person you admire told you they hate chocolate cake, you wouldn't buy them a chocolate cake. You would treat them according to what you know about them. In the same way, you treat *you* according to what you know about YOU. You will set up standards and boundaries to cater to your world. You will start new relationships or let some go, all because you have discovered one particular healthy component of you.

What's your favorite ice cream? What's your favorite holiday and why? What makes you cry? What makes you laugh? The very first step to discover your social self is to literally ask yourself questions a friend would ask to get to know you. You can ask 50 questions or 110 questions. Grab some paper or a notebook. You can even buy colored pens and a fabulous stylish notebook for this exercise. Or decorate it and make it creative on the outside. Title your notebook "Getting to Know Me" or something else creative and write your name on it. You can even make a playlist of encouraging music to listen to as you write and answer your questions. As I did this exercise, I listened to a playlist of positive songs that uplifted me.

Write out all your questions first, make space in between, then go back and take your time to answer each one. Think through thorough answers. Pretend you are being interviewed by someone who really wants to get to know you. Have fun with it. Make it a personable, exciting exercise. I suggest writing out at least eighty questions. Ask yourself about your present and future state of life. Where do you want to be in five years? What kind of relationship would you like to have? Use the internet to develop more questions.

Make sure to also write out at least ten questions that cater to what you want to be free of, in regard to your insecurities. Remember, I asked myself some specific questions about my skin condition and how I could move from allowing it to stop me from progressing. I answered the questions and then acted on them. You can do the same. Act on your responses and watch your life change. Also, consider grabbing an accountability partner and having them create their own questions and answers with you. Either way, don't just read this segment. Plan to do the work.

We get to know others by asking questions. We listen to their answers, and then we treat them accordingly. It's time to treat you according to the right perspective of you. Don't wait for others to tell you who you are: you discover you for yourself. Get to know yourself socially.

Discovering Your Intellectual Self

Remember when that kid threw a chair at me in chapter 5? I was over it! That same day, I sat at the cafeteria table and wrote out my innate gifts and talents before I walked in and terminated my contract with the elementary school. It wasn't long before doors opened for me to utilize my gifts and talents at the juvenile prison, my desired field. Going to the prison and interacting with the girls, especially with Chrissy, helped me fall out of love with how I looked and in love with who I was. This was all because I discover this component: I got to know my *intellectual self*.

Knowing your *intellectual self* is an important component. What is the benefit? To get to know you intellectually simply means to be aware of all your gifts, talents, and capabilities. What are you good at doing? What comes naturally to you? Knowing you intellectually will help you discover your purpose. Your purpose is big. You were created to do amazing things on earth.

Whatever your gift is, *you* are illuminated when you *utilize* your gifts and talents. Your beauty comes alive! Nothing else (especially superficially) matters. Your gifts and talents expressed to others become gifts back to you, because you experience an innate beauty that will last. It's true. When you use your gifts and talents, you are operating in something that can't be reproduced, something only you can do. Try it! Operate in what you are gifted at and watch what happens.

The very first step to discover your intellectual self is to simply become aware of your gifts, talents, and abilities. Think about what comes easily to you, even though it's hard for others. Think about what you love to do and would do for free! It could be something as simple as cleaning or doing math problems or organizing. You can also ask a friend or family member their thoughts on your gifts.

Take out your creative workbook and a pen or pencil, and list your gifts and talents. List them all, even the ones that do not seem important to you. After you've listed your gifts, complete the most important step of all: *use* at least one of your gifts. Grab an accountability partner and have them to help you move out on your talents.

Using your gifting doesn't have to be grandiose. Use it for someone in need. If it's baking, bake a cake for a homeless shelter. If it's listening and guiding others, start a teen book club or a kids club in your local community. (You could even use this book for a book club.) Not only will you see others experience your beauty, but you will too. Your focus will change. Your insecurities and worries about your image will vanish because you will be fulfilled in a way that's indescribable.

Once you have used your gifts, reflect on your experience. Write down how you felt, what it took to muscle up the energy to act on your gifts. How did you feel afterward? What were the reactions of others? How did you feel to see others happy and helped? If you're not much of a writer, you could vlog (video blog) about your experience. Share with others.

Whatever you do, don't stop using your gifts. Make it a habit, put a plan of action in place. What days will you act out on using your many gifts? Specifically, how will you do this? Don't use just one; use as many as you feasibly can. Apply for a job that allows you to use them. Pick a major in college to utilize your gifts. Make money using your gifts. All this will cause you to see *beyond* your physical state. You will begin to build on something that really matters—substance. Discover your intellectual self!

Discovering Your Emotional Self

Third, I discovered my *emotional self*. My journey was difficult, and throughout it, I felt so many emotions. I needed to learn what was emotionally healthy for me and accept nothing that was unhealthy.

To know you emotionally is to be aware of your feelings. The first step to discover your emotional self is to become aware of abnormal or irrational feelings. I noticed when I was depressed, and I noticed when I became suicidal. I took noticed of who I wanted to hang around and who I didn't want to hang around. I also noticed my happiness as I expressed my passion for teens. I took notice of my feelings and didn't ignore them or dismiss them.

My past experience of depression taught me not to allow negative emotions to linger and not to be afraid to ask for help. I found myself in bathrooms, in my car, or in my apartment, alone and crying about what I desperately wanted to change. I learned to get back up and not allow negativity to stay in my head. I then put barriers up to help me avoid dwelling on my hurts and pain. I decided to talk it out with my friends and with my cousin. But the biggest tool I utilized to help me become emotionally healthy was that I only hung around those who accepted me just the way I was *physically* and pushed me to be better *inwardly*. Only then did I finally allow others into my life, to assess me emotionally. I learned to accept what I was going through as I allowed myself to cry, but I got back up, knowing deep down that in all things I have a purpose for existing.

To discover your emotional self, become aware of when you are sad, happy, mad, glad, and so on. Notice how long you are sad, who or what brought you into that sadness, and how you come out of that state. Here are my two suggestions to help stop negative thoughts from lingering. First, when you think a negative thought, speak aloud a positive comment or truth. For example, if you silently think, "Man, there is no way I can be as good as she is!" say aloud, "I am uniquely gifted and talented. I can do anything that I put my mind to with excellence." You might consider using your notebook and writing out all your negative thoughts, leaving room beside them to write out positive thoughts or the positive truths that will dispel every negative idea. When I have done this, I would often use Scriptures to combat each negative thought. For example, I wrote out, "I feel ugly." Right beside it, I wrote, "The truth is, I am fearfully and wonderfully made. Marvelous are Your works that my soul knows well. God declares I am beautiful (Psalm 139:14)." Another example: I wrote out, "I'm not smart enough to do this!" Right beside it, I wrote, "The truth is, He stores away sound wisdom for the righteous (those who are in right standing with Him); He is a shield to those who walk in integrity (those of honorable character and moral courage (Proverbs 2:7, AMP)." God got me!"

Second, to stop negative emotions from lingering, tell someone you trust about them. Communicate that you want to stop thinking negatively and ask for help to stay accountable. Talk to a school counselor, especially if you don't trust anyone among your friends or family.

A therapist is trained to help you become more aware of the root causes of your actions. Let go of any negative stereotypes about seeing a "shrink." Therapy doesn't mean you're crazy. Going to a counselor means you are emotionally aware of the state that you are in and that you are wise enough to seek help. That's a good thing. View seeing a therapist as an investment in yourself. When you desire to become your best self, you invest in the positive things that will help you get to that place.

Allowing negative thoughts to linger can be highly destructive. Too many young kids, teens, and adults have ended their lives. No matter what you are going through, attempting to end your life is not the answer. The truth of the matter is, your story will change, just as seasons change. Live to see the story change. There is hope, and hope is all around you. How do I know? Because you are still living and breathing, and that means God has a purpose and plan for your life. Again, LIVE to see how the story ends. You are reading my book because I didn't succumb to ending my life to escape my emotional pain.

If you are thinking about ending your life, please call the National Suicide Prevention Hotline, 1-800-273-8255, or go to https://suicidepreventionlifeline.org/.

Discovering Your Spiritual Self

This has to be one of my favorite components of them all—and the most important: I discovered my *spiritual self*. In chapter 12, I mentioned that during college my sister would catch me awake at 4 a.m. reading my Bible. She had no clue as to what had happened. I never told anyone. I simply just wanted to get to know the God who regulated and healed my mind. So, from that day on, I started reading my Bible. I didn't realize I was building a foundation within me to know who I was spiritually. That foundation would give me a hope for the future, especially during my darkest times of dealing with a skin condition. I didn't know that such a season was around the corner.

To know you spiritually is to know and understand the One who created you. According to Genesis 1:27, God created all of humankind in His image. It is vital that we get to know the image that we were created in. Why? Here is an example: Have you ever bought a device and wanted to learn how to use it thoroughly? Who did you contact or go to? Have you ever had a phone, a car, or any other material thing break down? Who did you trust the most to fix it? We seek and trust the manufacturers of the item, right? Why? Because they built the very item we purchased, and they know it best. In the same way, our Creator knows us best. God, our Creator, is our manufacturer. He created us for a purpose. And in order to understand who we are and our purpose in life, we should seek and trust our manufacturer.

This is how you build your hope. This is what gives you validation to firmly know who you are. No other opinions of you matter; God knows you best. The Bible teaches us that God has developed a plan for our lives and that there is a plan for us to prosper holistically. Jeremiah 29:11 says, "'For I know the plans I have for you,' declares the Lord, "plans to prosper you and not to harm you, plans to give you hope and a future'" (NIV). What is that plan? What does that future look like? Only our Creator can reveal that to us.

I would like to share with you the things I did (and still do) to grow closer to God. My hope is that you will take from my experiences what you need to help you. I simply prayed and invited God (Jesus) into my heart. Romans 10:9 says, "If you declare with your mouth, 'Jesus is Lord,' and believe in your heart that God raised him from the dead, you will be saved" (NIV). I didn't have to pray a long prayer or go to a long church service to become a Christian. I just prayed a simple prayer of invitation.

Second, I was blessed to have parents who brought me up in a Bible-teaching, fun church with a thriving children and youth ministry. I didn't mind going to church as a kid or as a teen. As an adult, when I moved away I did the same thing; I joined a fun, thriving Bible-teaching church to learn more about God. I still enjoy being around like-minded individuals at church, and I love going to gatherings, classes and events put on by the church. Attending such things empowers and inspires me; it helps me to develop my spiritual component. I also got involved with ministries at church that allowed me to use my gifts (giving me a chance to see and experience my intellectual component even more).

When you find a church home, don't just go; get involved. One of the biggest benefits of going to a church or church events is finding a sense of community. That's how I met Leslie, Christina, and Madel. Church is basically where I found my husband. Now, how about that! When you get involved, you can surround yourself with like-minded individuals who are also growing.

Third, there is one thing I wish I would have done earlier —it might have saved me from much turmoil—but I do this step more now than ever: I read my Bible. As a kid, I would go to Sunday School, and we would learn about many Bible stories. However, I never read them for myself. So, when I finally started reading the Bible, I started with the stories. As a result, I really got to understand my Creator, my manufacturer: His power, His love, His nature. The more I read God's Word, the more I understood the *truth* versus a lie. We will always hear negative things and see negativity. But the more we read God's Word, the more we are reminded of the truth. For it is the truth that sets us free from all things negative (John 8:31–32).

Fourth, I consistently listen to positive music, messages, and sermons. We live in the age when we can listen to or watch digital media on most devices. Therefore, I play audiobooks, sermons from YouTube (by admired pastors), and Christian music on a constant basis. Now, I do have balance. On my music playlist you will find all genres of music from the best in the world, but you will see overwhelmingly more positive music and messages than anything else. This is a choice I made during the beginning of my journey as I discovered me. Listening to other leaders, preachers, and musicians has played a part in helping me develop my spiritual muscle—my spiritual component.

I advise you to take the same steps. Get to know your Creator. Build your firm foundation that will ignite a hope in you for life. Realize the plan and future that God has developed for you by discovering your spiritual self.

Discovering Your Physical Self

This you already know: we have a *physical component*. My skin improved over the years since the skin condition first occurred in 2002 when I was twenty-two years old. I took a good look at me and examined how I could personally take my health to another level, along with medicines when needed. Was I really eating the foods that could bring me total healing? Was I exercising as I should, to get my blood pumping? I started to educate myself and do my part. Eating salads out of the bag wasn't enough, and it wasn't the healthiest diet. Lesions on my face communicated to me that something was wrong on the inside. So I listened to my body and changed my unhealthy habits. I had to learn to treat my physical body right. The lesions on my face lessened more and more. I'm still learning how to be my healthiest self physically. Every day I strive to eat right and exercise—not to *look* my best but to *be* my best.

Now, just because I started taking care of my body, it doesn't mean I became physically perfect. I still had to deal with the scarring and skin indentions the lesions caused. How would I still like and love myself physically when I was nowhere near physical perfection? The truth is, when I began developing my social, intellectual, emotional, and spiritual self, I viewed my physical body from a different perspective, from a different set of lenses. How I looked no longer was—and still isn't—my main priority; being my best self became my focus. I wanted to feel healthy from the inside out to carry out my purpose. That's what mattered to me. As a result, I automatically accepted my imperfections. I accepted me physically.

Now, I truly understand the society we live in. Today, social media is prominent. We can tap and click our way into anybody's present life, whether it's honestly portrayed or not. Images are created for us to see perfection, excluding every single flaw, on a daily basis. In the middle of this, what do you do? Here is what I do. First, I remember the truth about beauty, no matter who or what challenges me to believe differently. But in order for me to put myself in remembrance of what true beauty really is, I stay away from the things that make me feel like I should focus on my outer appearance. I monitor what I put in front of me. For example: I'm not on social media as much. I limit my screen time to three days a week. And when I *am* on social media, I make sure to only follow what inspires, motivates, and encourages me. I don't follow people who are vain or self-absorbed, and I don't watch TV shows or other media outlets where that's the focus. Yes, I like makeup, and I love getting my hair and nails done. I have a balance. However, perfection is not my focus. I still accept me with my flaws. My flaws do not change my purpose, and my purpose is most important to me.

Second, I hang around individuals who know their purpose in life. My friends are not consumed with their appearance; they are consumed with their purpose in life. We gather to talk about what we are working on to change the world, what we watch that inspires us, and what we do to keep motivated. That's our mind-set. We strive to stay healthy so we can be in the best shape to fulfill life's purpose. Body image distortions are lessened when you are surrounded with positive people and positive thinking.

When you discover who you are socially, intellectually, emotionally, and spiritually, you will feel and see a difference in you physically. You will be motivated to become healthy on the inside so you can accomplish what you were created to do on the outside. Starting this journey will help you become successful and effective, because you will begin to live purposefully. Your mind-set will grow to another level, and you will stop caring or worrying about that which will fade. This means your focus will be on what God created you to do: to fulfill your purpose on earth.

I like to remind you that discovering true beauty is kind of supernatural. It's not dependent on your body type, skin tone, body size, or length of hair. Real beauty was created by your Creator, by a God who wonderfully made you (Psalm 139:14). *To know your physical body is to honor the gift of your life.* This component of you was given to you to carry out purpose, not to be admired just for looks and likes.

It is important to discover you. You possess a beauty that

has never been seen, and there will never, ever be another person like you. Your true beauty is an answer to others. *You being you is a gift to the world.* My hope is that you will discover the *gift* of you like I finally discovered the gift of me.

CHAPTER 20

PRESENT-DAY JOURNEY

Recently, I went to visit my dermatologist in Atlanta. As I write this chapter, I just finished a regimen that's supposed to eradicate acne for life. At my visit, the dermatologist congratulated me on my completion of the regimen and mentioned that she could give me treatments that could alleviate some of the scarring on my face but unfortunately not all. She said I would live with permeant scarring from the damaged that was done during those years acne. She said it carefully, seeming to prepare herself for my tears.

But I didn't cry. I didn't even think about crying. I said, "Okay, Doc. I understand." She appeared shocked and startled. It hit me that every day she sees clients who are desperate to get to a place called Pretty—a place of physical perfection. I was once that kind of client. But today, I continue to practice what I've learned. Knowing the truth about beauty really does set a person on a path to freedom from insecurities. I love this lifelong, life-changing journey. It has brought me so much freedom, purpose, and fulfillment.

We live in a world today where girls are opting out of going to college—not to go to work, not to save their money to start a business or pay for college, but to save money to get breast implants, butt injections, skin-lightening procedures, or tummy tucks. It's very disturbing. Many aren't even aware that going after physical perfection is a problem. This is because people truly believe in society's view of beauty. But society's definition of beauty is unrealistic. No one on this earth is perfect. No one. Yet every type of procedure is marketed to help you get to perfection. Getting to a healthy place is one thing, but trying to get to a place called Pretty will eventually fail you. Our bodies were created to inevitably age. But our purpose on earth, what we do with our existence here in this place—that will last forever.

Discovering who you are is a beautiful journey that should continue for life. Never stop growing, never stop developing. I challenge you to "be-*you*-tiful," and watch your world change for the better. You now know just how to be-*you*-tiful. So go ahead: start the journey.

We were created in the image of the One who created beauty. So be authentically you, and display true beauty.

To discover you is to discover true beauty.

To contact me
E-mail: Chara@TheTruthAboutBeauty.me
Social Media: @CharaMcGill

ACKNOWLEDGMENTS

I would like to take the time to thank everyone who helped me on this journey.

To my number one supporter—my husband Johnathan McGill. Babe, there would be nothing to tell, nothing to boast about, if it wasn't for your love. Thank you for seeing me in the ugliest season of my life. Thank you for loving me unconditionally. Thank you for believing in my dream from the first day we met. You have been so patient with me, even when I made all kinds of irrational decisions while chasing a dream. You only loved me more, to help me see the process clearly. I will love you forever.

Daddy! My executive coach. I did it! You made this book possible. Words can't express how much I love you and thank you. I will always be a daddy's girl. I'm honored to bear your name. Charles and Chara forever.

Mommie—to the lady in the pretty pink dress. I'm not sure if you know this, but Mom, you're still the most beautiful person in the world to me. Thank you for understanding me and approving my story.

To my twin sister, Tara. Girl, I tried not to tell your business. LOL! I love you so much. I've always admired your confidence and security. Thank you for allowing *me* to be *me* throughout my journey and throughout the countless days of comparisons. You're my ready-made best friend.

Zee—my oldest sister. I will forever look up to you. You're the best big sister ever. I know I've made you proud and that alone means so much to me.

Amber—my baby sister, aka my agent, aka my accountant, aka my prayer partner. Get your travel shoes ready. We've been dreaming of this moment for a while. Let's change the world.

To my "aunties from the East Coast" (I love when you two say that)—Aunt Jeanie and Auntie Trice-ie! You both have been such a blessing to me. You've taken over to plan my wedding when I didn't know what to do (because I wasn't expecting to get married); you've helped me with the production company to brand this book and message. Every visit, every phone call, and every time I see your face, you truly enhance my life. I thank you two for loving me through this season and for helping me find a love for myself that was lying dormant inside of me the whole time. Thank you for everything.

To my cousin Crystal: I know you think I'm playing when I say that I truly admire you. Well, I need you to know that I do. I admire your discipline, your strength, and your genuine heart of love. You told me that you're proud of me, and it meant the world to me. Thank you.

To my cousin Renata Scott. Cuz, you made the book! In such a low season of my life, God used you tremendously to be a blessing to me. I wouldn't go around family at all until you showed me what acceptance looked like. Thank you so much for accepting me. #AlwaysSisters.

Aunt Bren! Thank you for allowing me to just "show up" any time of the day. Your house became my safe haven. And even though I am in my thirties and married, I still feel like I can just show up anytime. That's love.

To Dr. Mae Henry: those rides to the prison and to other locations were more than just rides. I found my calling because you called. You're my favorite mentor.

Patricks! Shouting to the top of my lungs: "PATTY!!!!" I love you so much. I mean, what else can I say? The book tells it all. You're forever my little and big brother.

To Christina, Madel, and Leslie—aka two white girls and a Puerto Rican. First, thank you for approving the subtitle of that chapter. LOL! In all seriousness ... I need you three to know, you changed my world.

To Taryn Johnson ('Tee' in the book). Thank you for living out loud despite your imperfections. Because of you, I was inspired to live out loud as well.

To Jamila Jones. Your *yes* to discuss the truth about beauty alongside me sparked me to write. Thank you for opening up about your insecurities. You taught me to never judge people by what you see because you never know what others are going through.

To Ellie Alexander, my friend. Thank you for supporting me since the first day we met in Atlanta and walking with me to put out this book. I love seeing you. It means everything. #musicianwivesclub

Speaking of Atlanta ... to my ATL friends, Patrica Smith and Tiffany Beverly. I know you are glad that this book is done. I have blasted your ears off. Thank you for listening to me and for supporting me. I love you both so much.

To Cara Robinson—my ride-or-die. The first reader of the very first draft. Friend, I thank God for your life! And you know I speak many blessings over you. And they said you wouldn't make it past thirty. Singing HELLO to thirty-nine and goodbye to sickle cell.

To my mentor Faresha Sims. For the countless Audible books you've sent me, and the many lifetime subscriptions toward inspirational apps you've paid for, I can't thank you enough. Your financial investments and your wisdom have gotten me here. I'm grateful. Thank you always. Thank you for believing in me—and mostly, for pushing me.

To Pamela Lawson. Where do I start? Pam, you're the reason why this book is in print. Thank you for rearranging, suggesting, and editing my first draft. You're the best ever!

To Rebecca Miller, my professional editor. You're so perfect. So perfect. Thank you first for your services—but more than anything, for your words of wisdom, guidance, and encouragement. I will remember to embrace the red marks.

To Dr. Calvin Sims, my global coach. It's such an honor to call you friend. You're truly an answer to my prayers. I don't know how to thank you for your continuous support of this project. Thank you for pushing me to be my best self and for always reminding me not just of my inward beauty but also of my outward beauty.

To my foundational leaders, pastors, and mentors: Bishop Ronnie C. Crudup, Jacqueline Crudup, Pastor Joe Jackson, Pastor Henry Murphy, Pastor Henry Joseph, Bishop Garland Hunt, Pastor Eileen Hunt, Bishop Boone, Apostle, and First Lady Mussar. Where would I be without you? Thank you for following your calling. Because of your teachings, I'm still standing.

To all of the famous pastors, leaders, and inspirational speakers that I listen to: the late, great Dr. Myles Munroe; Touré and Sarah Jakes Roberts; Creflo and Taffi Dollar; Dr. I. V. and Bridget Hillard; Dr. Irishea Hillard; Dr. Tony Evans; Priscilla Shirer; Pastor Cynthia Brazelton; Albert Tate; Myleik Teele; Patrice Washington; Alan Hamilton; John Maxwell. Can't forget Guy Raz, Bishop T. D. Jakes, Stacia Pierce, Steve Harvey, ET ("the Hip Hop Preacher"), Lisa Nichols, Tiffany Pham, and Joshua Medcalf. Thank you. Your messages have pushed me to be here. I have so much more to do and will continue to listen to you.

To Duke TIP's class of 2019 of term 1 and term 2—fourth years. If you only knew how much you've encouraged me, inspired me, and pushed me, just by you just being you. The love you all displayed to me made my job easier. I was able to get up early in the morning to finish this project. Thank you, my loves. Never change. As always, I'll see you at the top.

And to all of my family and friends who I could not mention by name who walked with me, please know that I sincerely thank you so much. It's not me; it's space. I couldn't name everybody. But I love you all.

Rest in Love

To my Grandma: I imagine walking into your house and showing you my printed book. I can hear you when you first lay eyes on it, "Hey, Hey, Hey! Look out now!" You're smiling from ear to ear. You've ordered sixteen thousand copies before we could even sit. With tears streaming down my face, Grandma, I still believe that even in heaven angels are surrounding you, holding the book with you. Thank you for teaching me to never give up. I know you're proud of me.

To my aunt Melvene: I remember the week after you died, I would pull up to your house and sit in the car wondering what the next steps of my life would look like. I just needed a place of peace. I felt like you whispered, "Chara, God said to remind you that no eyes have seen, nor have ears heard, all that God has in store for you ... but ... I have seen it because he just gave me a glimpse. It's amazing if you just keep going." Thank you, Auntie. I know you're holding the book in heaven as well. Love you forever.

---

[1] A. M. Brausch and J. J. Muehlenkamp, "Body Image and Suicidal Ideation in Adolescents," *Body Image* 4, no. 2, (2007): 207–12

[2] Sarah Grogan, *Body Image: Understanding Body Dissatisfaction in Men, Women and Children*, 2nd ed. (New York: Routledge, 2008).

[3] S. J. Paxton, D. Neumark-Sztainer, P. J. Hannan, and E. Eisenberg, "Body Dissatisfaction Prospectively Predicts Depressive Symptoms and Low Self-Esteem in Adolescent Girls and Boys," *Journal of Clinical Child and Adolescent Psychology* 35 (2006): 539–49. See also A. M. Brausch and J. J. Muehlenkamp, "Body Image and Suicidal Ideation," 207–12.

[4] "About HIV/AIDS," Centers for Disease Control and Prevention, updated April 24, 2019, https://www.cdc.gov/hiv/basics/whatishiv.html.